INVESTIGATING

FINGERPRINTS

CRIME SCENE INVESTIGATORS

INVESTIGATING FINGERPRINTS

Hallie Murray and Chana Stiefel

Enslow Publishing
101 W. 23rd Street
Suite 240
New York, NY 10011
USA
enslow.com

Published in 2018 by Enslow Publishing, LLC.
101 W. 23rd Street, Suite 240, New York, NY 10011

Library of Congress Cataloging-in-Publication Data

Names: Murray, Hallie, author. | Stiefel, Chana, 1968- author.
Title: Investigating fingerprints / Hallie Murray and Chana Stiefel.
Description: New York, NY : Enslow Publishing, 2018. | Series: Crime scene investigators | Includes bibliographical references and index. | Audience: Grades 5-8.
Identifiers: LCCN 2017016452 | ISBN 9780766091856 (library bound) | ISBN 9780766095458 (paperback)
Subjects: LCSH: Fingerprints—Juvenile literature. | Criminal investigation—Juvenile literature.
Classification: LCC HV6074 .M87 2018 | DDC 363.25/8—dc23
LC record available at https://lccn.loc.gov/2017016452

Printed in China

To Our Readers: We have done our best to make sure all website addresses in this book were active and appropriate when we went to press. However, the author and the publisher have no control over and assume no liability for the material available on those websites or on any websites they may link to. Any comments or suggestions can be sent by email to customerservice@enslow.com.

Portions of this book appeared in the book *Fingerprints: Dead People Do Tell Tales.*

Photo Credits: Cover and interior pages (fingerprint) PRILL/Shutterstock.com; cover and interior pages (magnifying glass) azure1/Shutterstock.com; p. 6 Mr_Mrs_Marcha/Shutterstock.com; pp. 8, 22 Hulton Archive/Getty Images; p. 10 7505811966/Shutterstock.com; pp. 12-13 Ulrich Baumgarten/Getty Images; p. 16 Universal History Archive/UIG/Getty Images; p. 18 Tommy Flynn/Photographer's Choice/Getty Images; pp. 24-25 NEstudio/Shutterstock.com; p. 27 George Skadding/The LIFE Picture Collection/Getty Images; pp. 28-29 Kevin L Chesson/Shutterstock.com; p. 31 Kumpol Chuansakul/Shutterstock.com; pp. 32-33 Allen J. Schaben /Los Angeles Times/Getty Images; p. 35 518577181/Shutterstock.com; pp. 38-39 © David Giles/PA Wire/AP Images; pp. 42-43, 48 Philippe Psaila/Science Source; p. 50 Brendan Mialowski/AFP/Getty Images; p. 51 National Archives - JFK/Corbis Historical/Getty Images; p. 54 Bettmann/Getty Images; p. 58 st.noon/Shutterstock.com; p. 61 Hulton Archive/Archive Photos/Getty Images; p. 64 REUTERS/Alamy Stock Photo; p. 66 Kim Steele/Photodisc/Getty Images; p. 67 Andrew Brookes, National Physical Laboratory/Science Source; pp. 70-71, 75 © AP Images; p. 73 Greg Wahl-Stephens/Getty Images; p. 78 Designua/Shutterstock.com; p. 79 David Parker/Science Photo Library/Getty Images; p. 83 andresr/E+/Getty Images; p. 85 Justin Sullivan/Getty Images; p. 86 Lawrence Lawry/Science Photo Library/Getty Images; p. 89 Al Seib/Los Angeles Times/Getty Images; p. 91 franz12/ Shutterstock.com.

CONTENTS

NOT QUITE IDENTICAL

On May 1, 1903, police brought a convicted criminal named Will West to the federal prison in Leavenworth, Kansas. Although West claimed that he had never been there before, the guards were sure they recognized him. Since this happened before computers, the only way to check who was right was to look into the prison records.

The guards searched their files for "William West" and found him—but this William West was already serving a life sentence for murder. To make things even more confusing, the William West in the prison looked remarkably similar to the Will West who had just arrived. The guards were incredibly confused—what was going on?

At the time, police relied on body measurements to identify people. Each person was identified by a specific set of measurements,

A police officer in Paris in 1895 measures a man's foot, one of several specific body measurements used to identify people.

including their height, their head size, and the lengths of their arms, fingers, and feet. Not only did the two William Wests look the same, but they also had nearly identical body measurements. The guards now had two prisoners with the same name and the same appearance. How could they tell them apart?

Fortunately, the New York City Civil Service Commission, the New York State Prison System, and Leavenworth Penitentiary had all started using a new system of identification that year: fingerprints. Guards recorded the two men's fingerprints and the clerk found that their fingerprints were different enough to identify them as different people. Later research suggests that the two William Wests corresponded with the same family members, and another inmate said he believed they were identical twins who had somehow received the same name.[1]

Despite the fact that identical twins have the same genes—making their appearance and measurements virtually the same—they still have different fingerprints. Though the Will West story has become something of a legend in the field of crime investigation, it seems to have proved that fingerprints are a far better method of identification than measurements. Fingerprinting has remained a convincing tool for identifying criminals for more than one hundred years.

Fingerprints can be found everywhere, even in your own home. Fingerprints appear in smudges on the bathroom mirror, in sticky traces on the

Every time you touch something, you leave behind a piece of yourself in the form of fingerprints. You can see them on everyday items such as glasses, mirrors, and stainless steel appliances.

refrigerator, on a smooth computer screen, and on millions of other surfaces. The fact is, every time you touch a surface, you leave fingerprints behind.

Why do we have them? The truth is, scientists aren't really sure, although most believe that fingerprints developed to help us grip things when slippery or wet. They also seem to enhance our sense of touch, a discovery that engineers have used to help robots to more accurately feel pressure and texture.[2]

The most important question for crime scene investigators, though, is why fingerprints are so unique. Identical twins, for example, look the same, have almost the same measurements, and even have identical DNA, the molecular blueprint in cells that makes each person unique. Why aren't their fingerprints identical as well? Fingerprints take shape as a baby grows in its mother's womb and are already developed by their nineteenth week of existence. While the variety of patterns of fingerprints are partly determined by genes, fingerprints are also hugely affected by the movements of the baby's fingers inside the mother. Tiny movements affect the growth of dividing skin cells on each finger, causing subtle changes in fingerprints.[3] This explains why the fingerprints of identical twins, although similar, have distinct differences.

Because every person's prints are different, fingerprints have become essential clues in identifying criminals and solving crimes. Police have been

Police dust for fingerprints on a tile wall at a crime scene. The substance on the brush adheres to oils left by the fingerprints and helps make them visible.

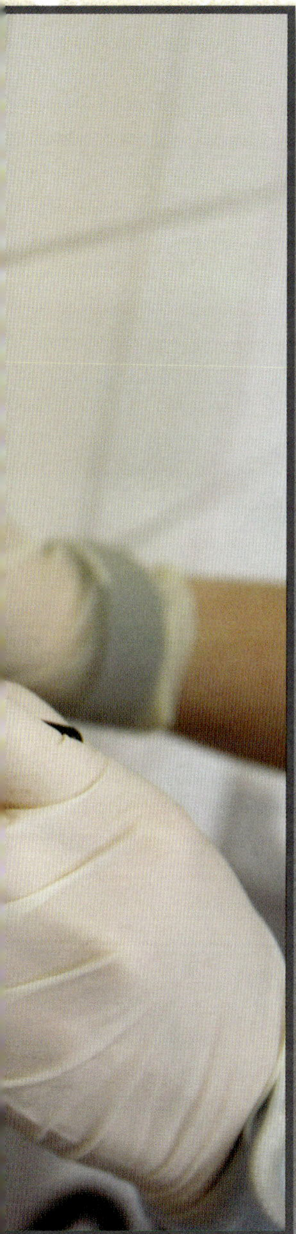

comparing fingerprints to nab criminals for more than a century. Matching a suspect's fingerprints to those found at a crime scene has developed as both an art and a science. In the past, detectives spent months comparing prints lifted from a crime scene to suspects' prints filed on note cards. Today computers narrow down the search and can help find a potential match in minutes. Fingerprint experts compare the prints closely and make the final call.

Since the early 1900s, fingerprints have helped solve millions of crimes. Today, they are used in conjunction with DNA and other evidence to help narrow down the list of suspects. Fingerprint analysis is not perfect—sometimes two people have fingerprints that are so similar it's impossible to decide who's guilty, while other times investigators are unable to find an entire fingerprint and have to determine the suspect's innocence using partial fingerprints. Still, it remains one of the most useful method of crime scene investigation, and it seems likely it will remain so for a long time.

CHAPTER 1

THE HISTORY OF FINGERPRINTS

Although fingerprinting in its modern incarnation has only existed for the past century or so, the idea that fingerprints can be used as identification is thousands of years old. A Chinese legal document from around 200 BCE—more than 2200 years ago—contains descriptions of using handprints as a kind of evidence. Three hundred years later, after the invention of paper, fingerprints were used commonly in China as signatures and continued to be used so until the end of the Tang dynasty in 907 CE.

The historical use of fingerprints as signatures has also been widely documented in Japan and India. Europeans, however, didn't seem to notice the uniqueness of fingerprints until German doctor J. C. A. Mayer's 1788 book, *Anatomical Copper-plates with Appropriate Explanations*, which contained drawings of various individual prints.[1] Less than a hundred years after Mayer's work was published, British officials began to use fingerprints to help identify criminals.

In India in 1858, Sir William James Herschel (1833–1917), a British government official, had workers "sign" contracts by inking and stamping their palms and fingerprints. Herschel used this technique because not all employees could sign their own names. In addition, those who could sign would sometimes deny that the signatures were their own. Over time, Herschel noticed that no two prints were the same. He also realized that a person's prints never changed with age. Herschel's print files became the first modern example in which fingerprints were used for the purpose of identification. Yet there was still a leap from signing contracts to solving crimes.

A New Method of Identification

In the late 1870s, a Scottish physician and missionary working in Tokyo, Japan, named Henry Faulds (1843–1930), became fascinated by fingerprints. Around 1878, he became interested in fingerprints left on ancient pottery that had been discovered at an archaeological dig near his hospital. Like Herschel, Faulds began collecting fingerprints of the people around him. He and his medical students also tried to rub off their fingerprints with knives,

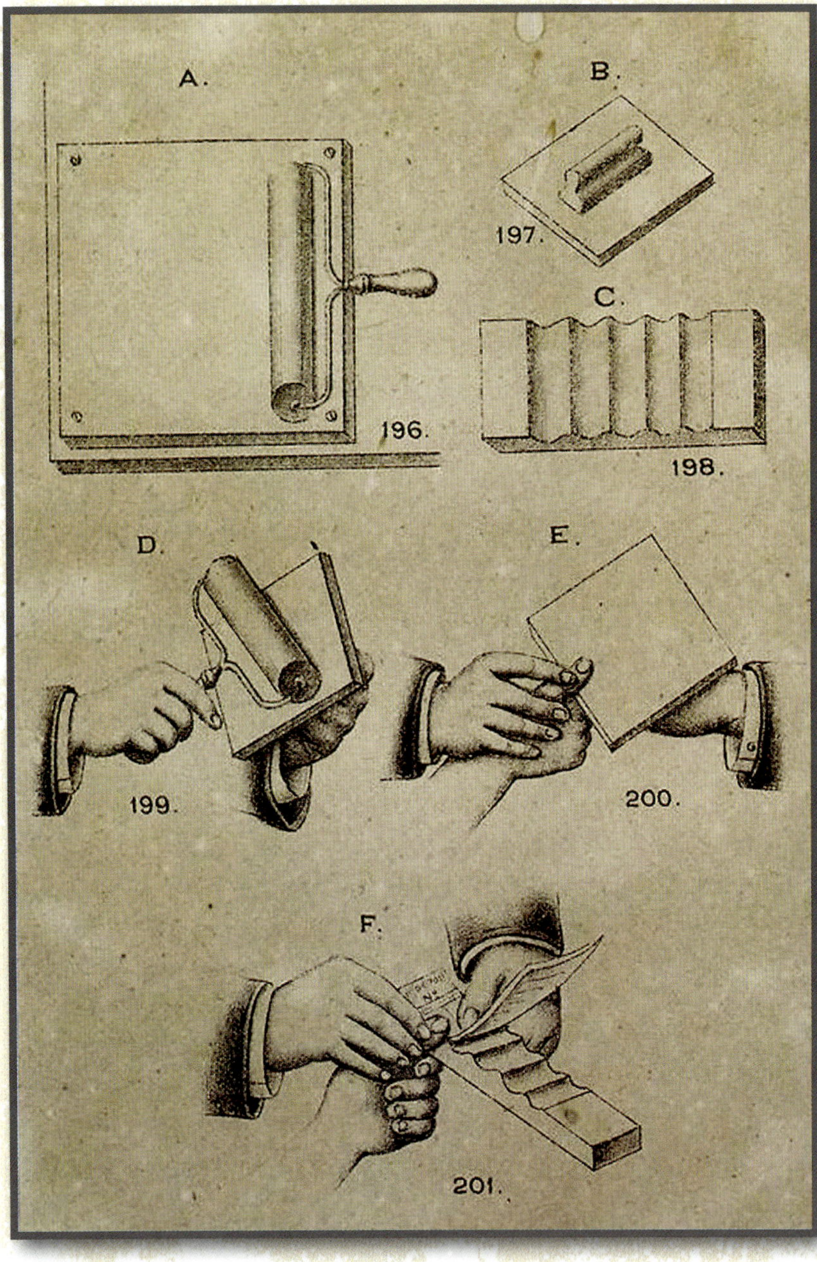

Juan Vucetich (1858–1925), an Argentine police officer, was a pioneer in the use of fingerprint identification. These explanatory diagrams accompanied his original instructions for taking fingerprints.

sandpaper, and other substances. They discovered that the prints grew back in exactly the same pattern as before.

Soon afterward, Faulds heard about a robbery. He used his newfound knowledge to help solve the crime. He even used fingerprints to prove a man's innocence. He showed police that a suspect's prints did not match a print found on the wall next to a building that had been robbed. In 1880, Faulds sent his observations to *Nature*, a prestigious British journal. "When bloody finger marks or impressions on clay, glass, etc. exist, they may lead to the scientific identification of criminals."[2]

Faulds was right on the mark. Although it took many years for Faulds to get credit for his work, it was only a matter of time before fingerprinting criminals caught on. As previously discussed, police in the late 1800s relied on a system of body measurements for identifying criminals. Then, in 1892, a British scientist named Francis Galton (1822–1911) became convinced that fingerprinting would be the wave of the future.

Galton came from a wealthy and well-known family of scientists. One of his cousins was Charles Darwin, who developed the theory of evolution by natural selection. Galton published a book called *Finger Prints* in which he described a detailed system of classifying fingerprints based on arches, loops, and whorls. He claimed that his fingerprint system could help identify military recruits, missing persons,

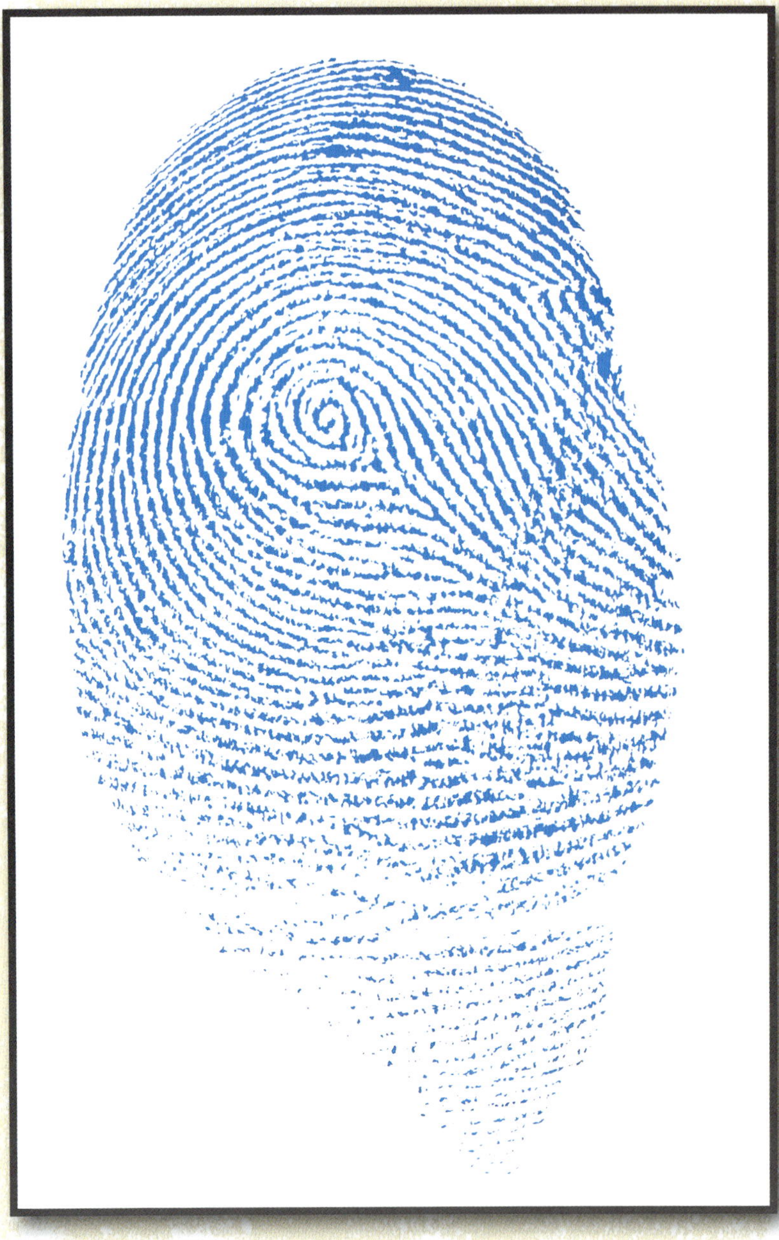

This close-up shows a fingerprint with loops in the center. It can be hard to see the loops, whorls, and arches on actual fingertips, but prints make these patterns much more visible.

and travelers. He also showed how investigators could save fingerprints found at a crime scene and later match them to prints from another case. Galton calculated that the odds of finding two people with identical fingerprints was one in sixty-four billion.

In 1900 Edward Henry (1850–1931), inspector-general of police in Bengal, India, published a book that made classifying fingerprints more user-friendly. *The Classification and Uses of Finger Prints* became very popular in police bureaus around the world. Henry's basic system, which was itself based in part by earlier descriptions of various fingerprints described by Czech physiologist Johan Evangelista in 1823, served as the basis for modern-day fingerprint classification until the 1990s.

The Henry system grouped prints based on loops, whorls, and arches. Each finger was assigned a number, beginning with the right thumb as number 1 and ending with the left pinky as number 10. Numbers were then assigned to fingers that had a whorl pattern. For example, if fingers 1 or 2 had a whorl pattern, they each received a value of 16. Fingers 3 and 4 each had a value of 8. Fingers 5 and 6 each had a value of 4. Fingers 7 and 8 each had a value of 2 and fingers 9 and 10 had a value of zero. Loop and arch patterns also received a value of zero.

The examiner then added the number values of whorls on even-numbered fingers and added one. Then he or she added the values for odd-numbered

Fingerprint Features

Arches, loops, and whorls have subcategories. An arch, for example, can be plain (rounded like a hill) or tented (pointed at the top like a traffic cone). Loops can either be ulnar (pointing toward the pinky finger) or radial (pointing toward the thumb). Whorls can have pockets, a tight swirl of ridges at the center. They may also form a double loop, a pattern in which two whorls collide in the center.

In addition to arches, loops, and whorls, there are several other features crime scene investigators use to examine and match fingerprints:

bifurcation The place where a ridge divides into two (also called a fork).

bridge A connecting ridge between two parallel running ridges.

core The approximate center of a fingerprint's ridge pattern.

delta A triangular ridge pattern where ridges divide.

divergence The place where ridges split apart after running parallel.

dot A ridge that doesn't display direction; its length approximates its width.

enclosure A ridge that splits and then rejoins.

end The point where a ridge starts or stops.

focal point An identical point of comparison between two fingerprints.

furrow The valley between the ridges.

island A small ridge section located between other, longer ridges.

ridge count The number of ridges that run between the core and delta focal points.

When studying prints, examiners begin by locating two focal points: a core and a delta. They then record the number of ridges between the core and delta, or between two deltas. A loop has one core and one delta. A whorl has two or more deltas. An arch has no core or delta.

The tiny variations in a fingerprint, such as cores and deltas, are called minutiae. Fingerprints can vary by the number, types, and positions of ridges and minutiae, making each fingerprint truly unique. In the United States, forensic labs differ on the number of corresponding points that are required to make a match between two prints. Some labs have made a match with as few as eight points. Most rely on about ten matching points. In England, experts must find sixteen corresponding points in order to make a match.[3]

This 1905 artwork depicts British police commissioner Sir Edward Henry, who developed a fingerprint classification system to identify criminals police departments used for nearly a century.

fingers, plus one. The examiner recorded the two sums as a fraction, for example 15/2. This individual's prints were then filed in a group of other prints that also received 15/2. The fraction 1/1 indicated that no fingers had whorl patterns. The fraction 32/32 showed that all fingers had whorl patterns. Categorizing fingerprints with a system like this cut down on the need to scour through every fingerprint on file.

Because of his work, Henry was appointed assistant commissioner of Scotland Yard (the London police) and head of the Criminal Investigation Department (CID). The CID opened a fingerprint bureau in 1901. The next year, relying on fingerprint evidence, the bureau arrested 1,722 repeat offenders. One can only imagine the excitement that must have spread when they discovered that number was nearly four times the number of repeat criminals that the body-measurement system had identified in its most successful year.

From Scotland Yard to the United States

In 1903 the New York City police department became the first in the United States to fingerprint suspects. At the World's Fair in St. Louis in 1904, fingerprint experts from Scotland Yard trained American police officers to collect and analyze fingerprints. Over the next few years, fingerprinting gradually became routine practice in police departments across America. In 1910 the first murder conviction in the United States based on fingerprinting occurred in Chicago: the killing of Clarence Hiller.

On September 18, 1910, before daybreak, Hiller awoke to find a stranger in his home. The two men struggled and tumbled down a flight of stairs. The intruder fired two shots, killing Hiller, and then fled. Soon afterward, police arrested a suspect, Thomas Jennings, less than a mile from Hiller's home. He was found carrying a loaded gun and was covered with bloodstains. Jennings claimed the blood had come from injuries he had gotten when falling from a streetcar.

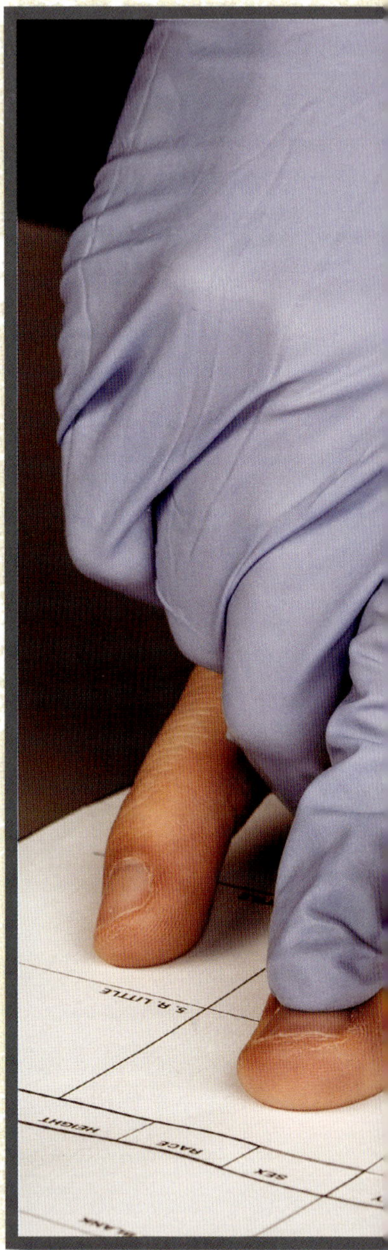

Police collected evidence at Hiller's home, including unused bullets and traces of gravel and sand. However, the key evidence that sent Jennings to jail was a set of fingerprints found in the kitchen. On the day before he was murdered, Hiller had painted some stair rails next to a window.

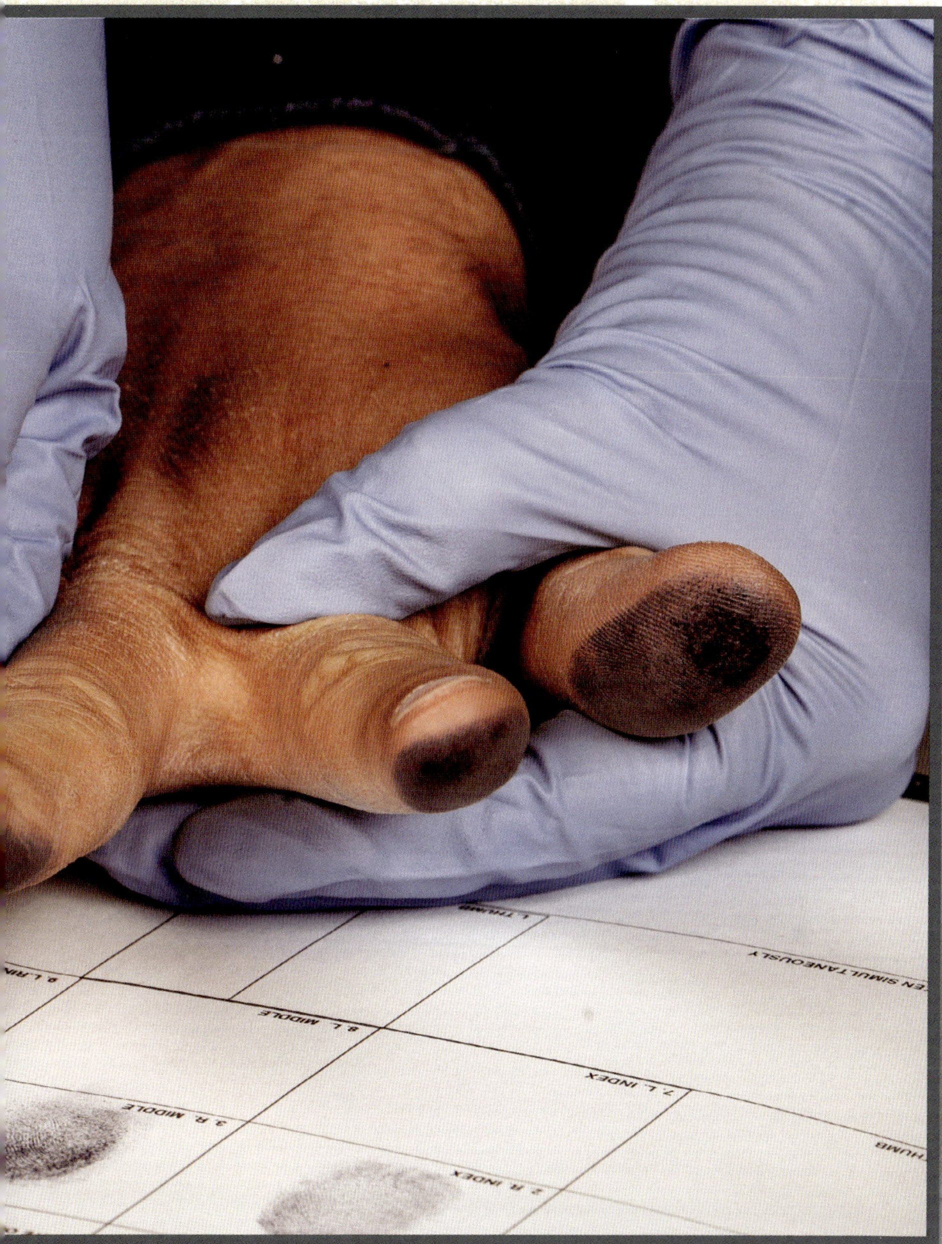

An official takes a person's prints the traditional way, using ink and paper. Today fingerprints are usually taken digitally.

When Jennings broke into Hiller's home through that window, he had touched the wet paint and left a set of four fingerprints.

The Chicago police department compared Jennings's prints to those found at the crime scene. They were a match. In 1911 Jennings was found guilty of murder and was executed. Before his execution, however, Jennings's lawyers tried to appeal his conviction. They challenged the Supreme Court of Illinois on the grounds that fingerprint evidence should not be accepted as evidence. In a landmark ruling, the Illinois Supreme Court stated, "There is a scientific basis for the system of fingerprint identification, and . . . the courts are justified in admitting this class of evidence."[4] Jennings's fate was sealed. His case made fingerprinting in criminal cases a more accepted practice around the world.

In 1924 Congress established the FBI's Identification Division to collect and catalogue fingerprint files from across the nation. For the first time, using the unique patterns in fingerprints, police could link a robber who had committed a crime in one place to a theft he had carried out in another place at a different time.

In the beginning, comparing fingerprints on notecards was a painstaking job. Sorting through thousands of fingerprints by hand could take months. Suspects were often released before a match could be made. Fortunately, in the 1960s, investigators began using computers to help match

A woman uses a magnifier to study and compare different sets of fingerprints in an FBI office in 1944.

fingerprints. In the 1970s, the FBI established the Automated Fingerprint Identification System (AFIS), a computerized system that collects criminal histories and provides automated fingerprint matches. In 1992 the Identification Division became the Criminal Justice Information Services Division.

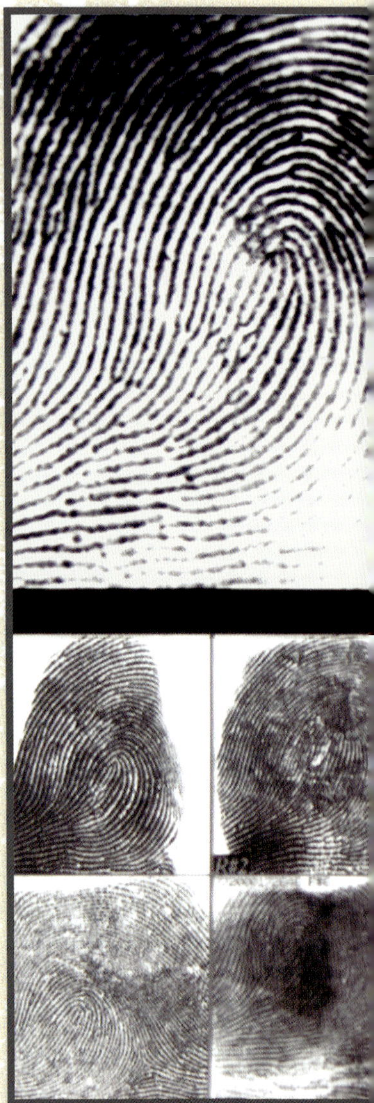

New Technology for the Next Generation

In 1999 the FBI cranked it up a notch. They began using the Integrated Automated Fingerprint Identification System (IAFIS), which joined together AFIS databases from around the country. IAFIS stored and exchanged fingerprint data 24/7 and eventually held the criminal histories of more than seventy-seven million people.[5] Several thousand new records were added every day, and for each search, computers ran through millions of possibilities and displayed the prints most likely to match. IAFIS cut down on the time it took to make a fingerprint match from months or weeks to hours

A fingerprint match comes up in AFIS, a computerized fingerprint database first used by the FBI in criminal investigations.

Fingerprinting in the Digital Age

The technique of obtaining someone's fingerprints is called dactyloscopy. The old-fashioned way to take a person's fingerprints just uses ink and a card. First, sweat and dirt is removed from the fingertips by wiping them with alcohol. Then, the ridge area is covered in black ink. Each fingertip is rolled onto a card from one side of the fingernail to the other. These prints are called rolled fingerprints. Next, the suspect presses down all ten fingers to make flat prints. Before computers, fingerprint cards were organized in filing cabinets according to their ridge patterns and mailed from precinct to precinct to identify criminals.

The modern, high-tech way to take fingerprints uses a digital scanner called Live Scan. A person lays his or her fingers flat on a scanner, where the scanner converts the fingerprints into a digital picture. A computer marks notable features of the fingerprints, including the whorls, arches, loops, and minutiae. Fingerprint scans are stored on the

FBI's nationwide database and can be shared instantly. Live Scan technology is now used at law enforcement agencies and private companies across the country, and fingerprints are used for many purposes outside of police activity. Everyone from teachers to healthcare professionals to lawyers may have their fingerprints taken by Live Scan to confirm a person's identity or to perform certain background checks.

In some workplaces, digital scanners are used instead of time cards to record an employee's hours. Fingerprints are no longer just for law enforcement.

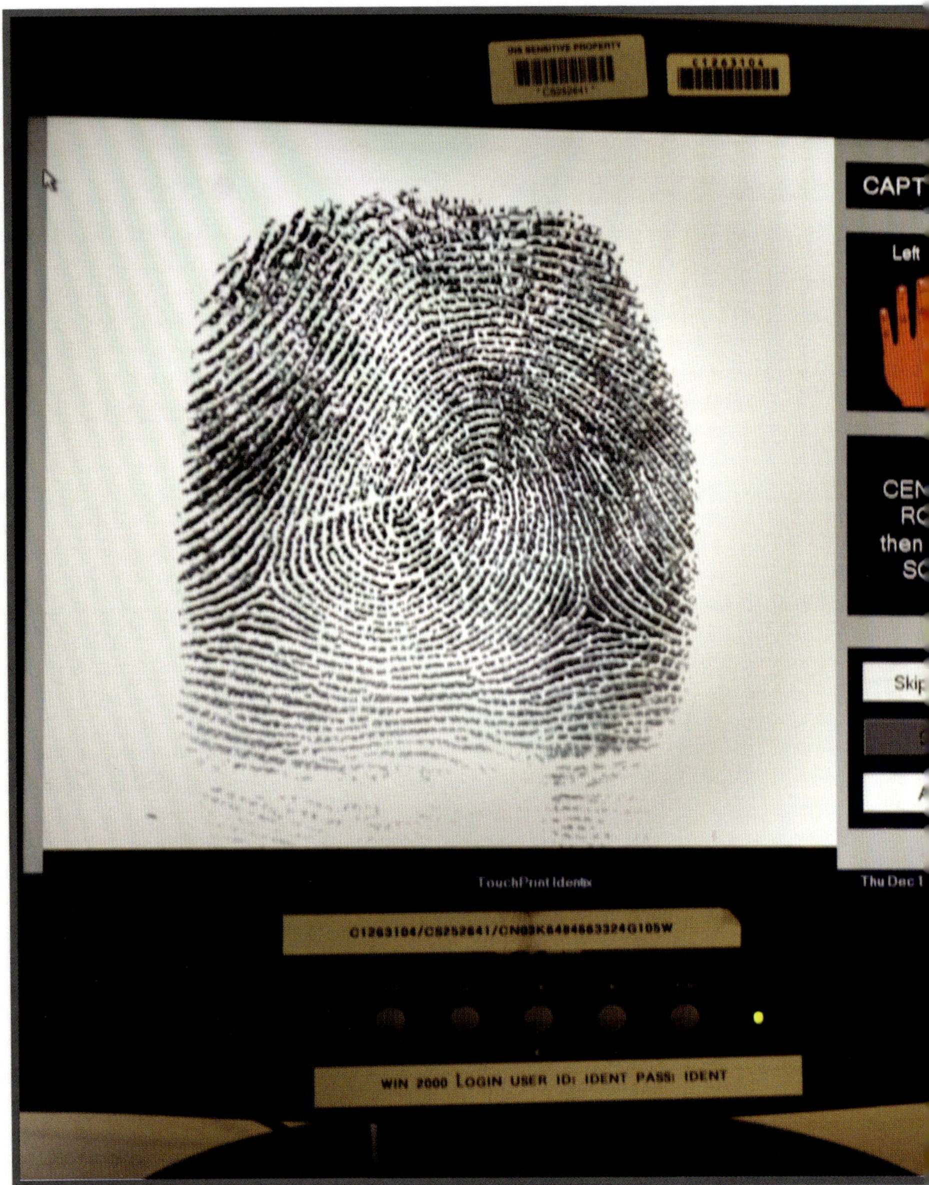

A fingerprint belonging to a fugitive is scanned into IAFIS. The system quickly identifies criminals by matching a live-scanned fingerprint with one stored in a national database.

and minutes. It could search latent, or partial, fingerprints or locate images through text-based searches. IAFIS was so effective that it soon was used to process far more data than it was ever designed for. Finally, the FBI decided to retire the system and replace it with a new system that could handle even more data and supported new technological advances in biometrics.

From 2010 to 2014, the FBI worked to implement their largest information technology system ever: Next Generation Identification (NGI). NGI replaced IAFIS and added a number of other biometric identifiers to the FBI's database. It was rolled out in six phases called "increments." Once all of these increments had been completed, IAFIS was decommissioned and no longer used. Increment 1, completed in 2011, was the implementation of Advanced Fingerprint Identification Technology (AFIT), which replaced the AFIS part of IAFIS. AFIT

What Are Biometrics?

The word *biometrics* comes from combining the prefix *bio*, which has come to mean "organic life," and *metrics*, meaning "measurements." Biometrics are any kind of measurable characteristic that can be used to identify a person. They are usually split into two categories: "physiological" and "behavioral."

Physiological identifiers have to do with body shapes, like a very advanced version of early measurement techniques that unfortunately were no help in identifying the two Will Wests in the introduction. Modern physiological biometrics include fingerprints or palm prints, facial recognition, DNA analysis, iris or retina scanning, and chemical markers in a person's unique scent. Behavioral biometrics have to do with the way someone acts or moves, such as the individual's gait, or walking pattern, and his or her voice.

Biometrics are becoming more and more common for security purposes: most smartphones have fingerprint technology, and there are a number of apps that use vocal or facial recognition on top of fingerprints. Other biometrics are already used in secure government spaces or for advance crime-solving techniques, and they have led to a whole host of new legal issues about privacy. Just how much should the government be allowed to know about the bodies of its citizens?

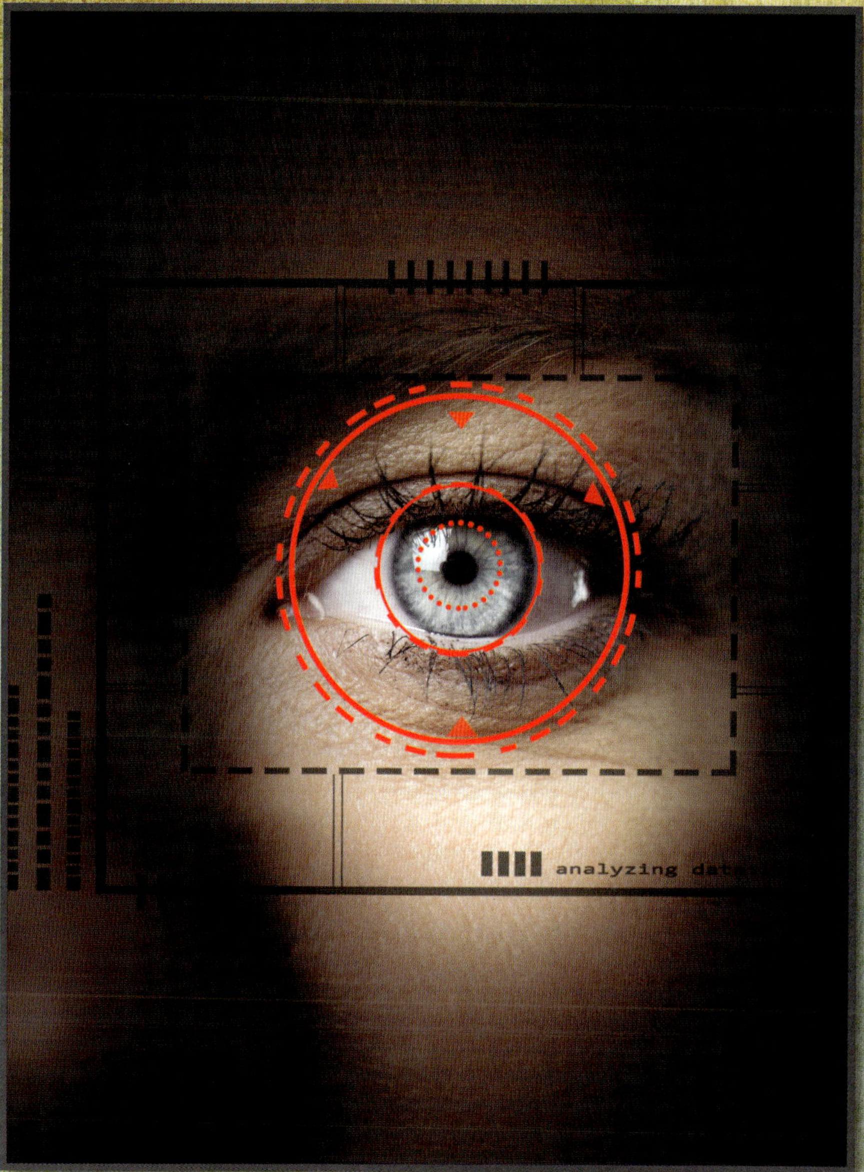

Retina scanning is a type of physiological biometric that can be used to confirm someone's identity.

increased matching accuracy from 92 percent to more than 99 percent, and response times became even shorter. Increment 3, Latent and Palm Prints, was completed in 2013 and made latent print searches three times more accurate than they had been with IAFIS. This increment also allowed searches of unsolved prints and encouraged agencies to submit palm prints along with fingerprints to increase the amount of searchable data available.[6] Thanks to the NGI system, fingerprinting is now more effective and efficient than ever.

CHAPTER 2

PICKING UP PRINTS AT THE SCENE OF THE CRIME

Terrorism is the use of violence to intimidate a government or group of people, especially violence against bystanders who cannot necessarily effect change themselves. The most common example of terrorism against the United States cited today is 9/11, when two hijacked airplanes flew into the twin towers of the World Trade Center in New York City on September 11, 2001. But terrorism is a tactic that has been used for centuries by violent political groups hoping to make more powerful groups listen to them.

The Irish Republican Army is a group that was very active in the twentieth century and believed that all of Ireland should be independent. They committed a number of terrorist attacks against the United Kingdom with the goal of liberating Northern Ireland. One such attack was the 1996 Docklands bombing, where an explosion from a truck bomb ended up killing two people, injuring thirty-nine more, and causing more than two hundred million dollars in damage.

Police officers weren't sure they would be able to solve the case—all that was left of the shopping area was a large crater, leaving very little evidence. But thanks to some luck, ingenuity, and the magic of fingerprints, Scotland Yard finally cracked the case.

Trailing Triple Thumbprint Man

Initially, the only lead the Docklands bombing investigators had was a police officer who had seen the truck before it exploded. When newspapers published a picture of the truck, one witness called to say he had seen the vehicle parked 10 miles (16 kilometers) from the bomb site just days before the blast. Two men had been seen unloading a trailer that the truck had been hauling.

Investigators found the trailer parked in an empty lot. Next to it was a tire filled with garbage in which investigators found a chart that tracked the truck's travels from England to Northern Ireland and back. Police also traced the trail back to a motel in Carlisle, England, where the bombers had apparently stayed twice.

Investigators combed the motel for evidence. Although the rooms had been cleaned since the

This photo was taken at the site of the February 9, 1996, Docklands bombing eight months after the attack took place.

bombing, detectives checked for fingerprints. As in any crime scene, the investigators knew that prints could be left on virtually any surface.

At the motel in Carlisle, England, detectives uncovered one hundred prints. Then they fingerprinted the motel's staff to rule them out as suspects.

Three Types of Fingerprints

There are three kinds of fingerprints investigators might find at a crime scene: *Plastic prints* are 3-D, molded impressions of prints left in clay, soap, wet paint, wax, wet cement, or other soft or sticky materials.

Patent prints are visible to the naked eye. These are the smudgy fingerprints left by dirty or sweaty fingers. Patent prints can usually be photographed or lifted with special tape.

Latent prints are invisible and may be found on glass, plastic bags, paper, or any number of surfaces.

One latent thumbprint, found on an ashtray, gave investigators a lead. It didn't match any of the motel staff.

To uncover the print, the investigators used a technique called superglue fuming. Superglue is strong, fast-acting glue made from an adhesive called cyanoacrylate. Chemicals in the glue stick to amino acids (proteins) left on a surface by a fingerprint. Technicians place the object under investigation in an airtight tank along with a small heater.

They put a few drops of superglue in a dish, seal the tank, and crank up the heat. As the superglue heats up, it turns into a gas. Its particles stick to the amino acids in a fingerprint. The result? A visible fingerprint coated in white residue appears. The dried glue makes it hard to smudge. Investigators dust on some powder to make the print stand out even more.

The superglue-enhanced thumbprint found on the ashtray at the motel in Carlisle gave investigators their first clue. Meanwhile, other investigators had been carefully sorting through the garbage found near the trailer. They discovered a meal voucher from a ferry that had carried the truck from Northern Ireland to England. No fingerprints were visible on the voucher, but it was possible that a suspect had touched it.

The problem is that porous (or absorbent) surfaces such as paper or cardboard absorb the sweat in fingerprints, leaving the marks invisible. The challenge is to make a latent print appear without destroying the paper. To accomplish this, investigators usually use chemical substances that react with other chemicals found in sweat. Two of these substances are called ninhydrin and DFO (or, as a chemist might call it, 1,8-Diazafluoren-9-one). Investigators either spray a piece of evidence with one of these chemical solutions, or dip it in one. Then they warm the evidence in an oven. Fingerprints treated with ninhydrin appear purple. Those

treated with DFO glow when lit by a laser or blue-green light. After treating the meal voucher with both ninhydrin and DFO, police uncovered a second clue—another faint thumbprint. It matched the print on the ashtray from the motel.

Surprisingly, a third matching thumbprint was found on a copy of *Truck & Driver* magazine. It had been left out in the rain near the trailer for two weeks. To uncover that print, lab techs used physical developer, a solution of silver and iron compounds. These compounds are known to reveal prints on porous surfaces that have been soaked in water.

Now Scotland Yard had three thumbprints from the same person, linking him to the bombing. They nicknamed their suspect "Triple Thumbprint Man." Hot on the trail, investigators ran the thumbprints through their computer database. No match was found. The IRA had chosen an operative with no criminal record. His thumbprints could not be traced. The investigation screeched to a halt.

Several months later, the British Army's Special Forces arrested a group of IRA terrorists suspected of carrying out sniper shootings. One of the shooters was James McArdle, a bricklayer and truck driver

A forensic scientist uses cyanoacrylate (superglue) fuming to see if there are any invisible fingerprints on this license plate.

from Ireland. Investigators ran McArdle's fingerprints through their computer system and compared them with the London bomber. They matched! James McArdle was the notorious Triple Thumbprint Man.

McArdle's trial in June 1998 laid out the details of the fatal bombing. Lawyers showed how the

A Myriad of Methods to Find Fingerprints

Since latent prints can't be seen without using special methods, crime scene investigators are trained to apply more than forty techniques to uncover and retrieve fingerprints without destroying them, including superglue fuming. They use a variety of powders, chemicals, gases, or special lights and lasers to expose them.

Dusting Powder

Surface: Nonporous (non-absorbent) surfaces, including walls, windows, doors, and furniture

Procedure: CSIs use soft brushes to dust a surface with a fine powder, such as finely ground aluminum. The powder sticks to the moisture left behind by oily, sweaty, or sticky fingers. Different colored powders make prints appear on different backgrounds.

Note: Some "handy" places to dust for prints: the rearview mirror of a car; the underside of a toilet seat (for men's prints); dirty dishes and silverware.

DFO (1,8-Diazafluoren-9-one)

Surface: Porous (absorbent) surfaces, such as paper or cardboard

Procedure: A laser or blue-green light is shone on prints treated with DFO, making prints glow. DFO is one hundred times more sensitive than ninhydrin, but ultraviolet (UV) light is needed to make prints treated with DFO appear.

Note: Adding heat improves results. If a lab oven is not available, investigators can use a toaster oven, hair dryer, or dry iron.

Gentian Violet

Surface: Sticky adhesives like tape and labels; wide variety of surfaces

Procedure: A solution of gentian violet is applied to a surface, dyeing dead skin cells or fatty deposits left by a fingerprint and making the print appear purple.

Note: Gentian violet contains phenol, which is poisonous and can be absorbed through skin. Experts must always wear gloves and protective clothing when handling this substance.

Continued on page 46

Continued from page 45

Alternate Light Sources (or Forensic Lights)

Surface: Multiple surfaces, including paper, fabric, and skin

Procedure: In a darkened room, investigators focus a laser on a surface. The light illuminates a fingerprint without altering the print or leaving any residue. Fluorescent powders sometimes help make prints more visible. One drawback is cost. One machine used in an FBI fingerprint lab costs $65,000.[1]

Note: This technique was discovered by accident. In the 1970s, Canadian researchers noticed that when they turned on lasers, their fingerprints kept getting in the way. Their annoyance turned into a major breakthrough for fingerprint detection.

Ninhydrin

Surface: Porous surfaces, including paper and cardboard; wallpaper

Procedure: Ninhydrin reacts with traces of amino acids in a fingerprint. Heat makes the process work faster. Sometimes technicians iron surfaces treated with ninhydrin to speed up the process. When lit up, ninhydrin makes prints appear purple.

Note: This technique has been in use since 1954. Ninhydrin is the most common chemical used for developing prints on paper. It has been used to develop prints that are more than fifty years old.

RUVIS (Reflected Ultraviolet Imaging System)

Surface: Most smooth, nonporous surfaces, including plastic bags, the sticky side of tape, glossy magazines, photographs, credit cards, compact discs, linoleum tile, etc.

Procedure: RUVIS works like a portable laser. It uses a special UV light to illuminate a print, which can then be photographed with UV-sensitive film.

Note: RUVIS can be used to find prints on skin.

Superglue (Cyanoacrylate) Fuming

Surface: Nonporous surfaces, including metal, glass, aluminum foil, rubber bands, Styrofoam, and plastic products; also some porous surfaces

Procedure: In an airtight space, superglue is heated in a beaker. The glue vaporizes. As it condenses, crystals stick to the oils or sweat in fingerprints, leaving a white residue that makes an image appear. Dyes or powders are often added to make the prints stand out.

Note: In 1978 the Japanese National Police Agency became the first to use superglue as an agent to make latent prints visible.

Fingerprints appear on paper after nihydrin is applied. Nihydrin bonds with the proteins in the sweat left by fingertips and turns purple during a reaction with heat.

bomber made trips from Ireland to England as a practice for the attack. Terrorists had packed the truck with more than a ton of explosives. The fingerprint evidence was enough to tie McArdle to the crime. On June 25, 1998, Triple Thumbprint Man received a sentence of twenty-five years in prison for "conspiracy to cause explosions." However, McArdle served only two years in prison. In 2000 he was released as part of a new peace agreement between the IRA and the British government.

When Mistakes Solve Murders

It is evident that crime scene investigators are trained to use a wide variety of techniques to uncover fingerprints. Their job is tricky because if they use the wrong technique they could end up destroying evidence. However, in at least one notorious case, a mistake in exposing prints led to the identification of an infamous killer.

November 22, 1963, was one of the darkest days in American history. On that day, during a parade in Dallas, Texas, President John F. Kennedy was assassinated. Police raced to find the killer. Less than two hours after the shooting, police found a rifle lying next to a window in the Texas Book Depository, a building that overlooked the parade route. Cardboard boxes were stacked around the window. The police checked for fingerprints. A right palm print was found on the rifle. Fingerprints also were found on the cardboard boxes and on a paper bag.

The prints matched a man named Lee Harvey Oswald. A complicating factor was that Oswald worked in the Book Depository building. He could have left the prints on the boxes and bag at any time. In addition, someone could have placed the rifle by the window to frame him. The police needed to prove that these were fresh prints left at the scene at the time when Kennedy was killed. Unlike some other kinds of evidence (such as a dead body), fingerprints can't be dated. That is, fingerprints can't tell you when a crime may have occurred. Yet in this case, something unexpected happened. Dallas detectives had made a mistake when they were checking for prints. Their mix-up, however, would lead to success.

Cardboard is a porous, or absorbent, surface—like paper. As explained in the London bomber case, the correct way to check for latent prints on cardboard is to treat it with chemicals such as ninhydrin. Yet the Dallas detectives used dusting powder by accident. Dusting powder is usually used only

A replica of Lee Harvey Oswald's rifle and a bunch of cardboard boxes sit near the window of the Sixth Floor Museum in the Dallas County Administration Building, which used to be the Texas School Book Depository at the time of Kennedy's assassination.

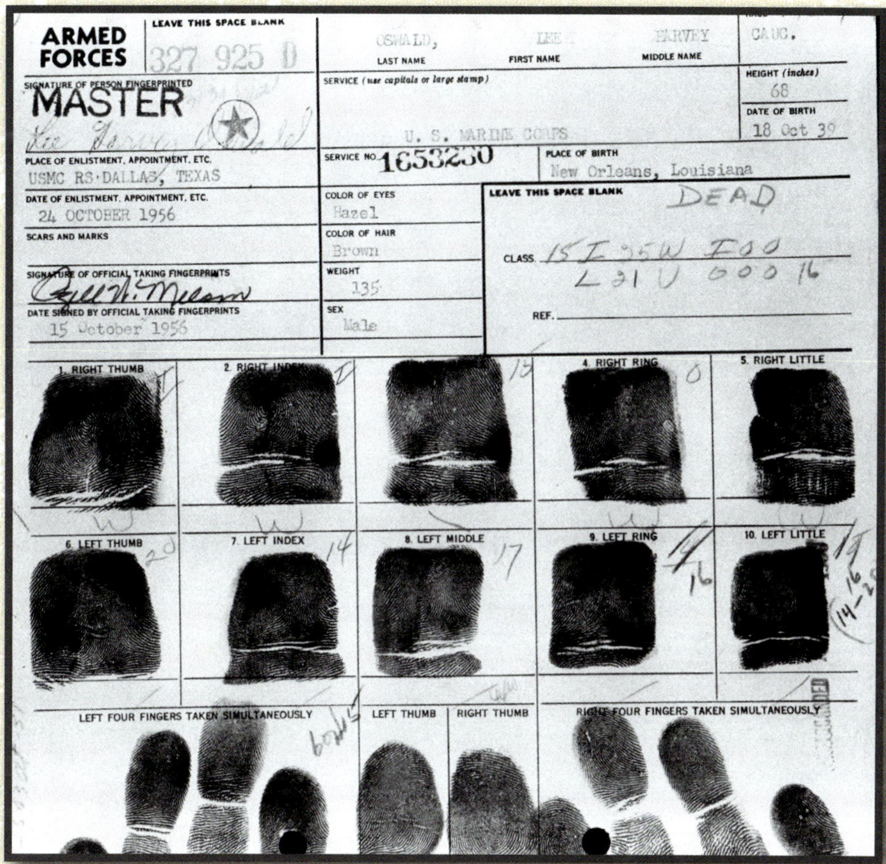

Lee Harvey Oswald's fingerprints were put on file when he applied to the US Armed Forces. His fingerprint record was later used as evidence in the investigation of the assassination of President Kennedy in 1963.

on solid, nonporous surfaces such as glass. Still, the detectives managed to uncover several prints. How did that happen?

Crime lab investigators in Washington, DC, examined the boxes more closely. They brushed dusting powder on similar boxes. To their surprise, the dusting powder uncovered fingerprints for up to three hours after prints had been left. After that, the cardboard absorbed the moisture in the prints, causing them to disappear. A lightbulb went off for the investigators: Oswald's prints were uncovered by police dusting the cardboard in the first three hours after the assassination. So Oswald had to have been standing at the window at the time Kennedy was killed. With other evidence mounting against Oswald, detectives knew he was their man.

You Can Run, But You Can't Hide

As one grows old, many things about his or her body changes, but not fingerprints! They stay the same throughout a person's entire life, which makes them a particularly good method of identification. If someone commits a crime at a young age and leaves a fingerprint behind, the person could still be connected to the crime years later because his fingerprints never change. That's exactly what happened to Valerian Trifa, who came to the United States from Romania in 1950. Trifa was among the masses of immigrants entering the country from Eastern Europe after World War II (1939–1945). He claimed he was a displaced person who had spent time in a German concentration camp.

Soon after his arrival in the United States, Trifa was ordained as a priest of the Romanian Orthodox Church. He rose to the rank of bishop and led a church of thirty-five thousand members in Grass

Lake, Michigan. In 1955 Trifa gave an opening prayer before the US Senate. He became a citizen of the United States in 1957. He later became an archbishop.

But Trifa had a dark and hidden past. Dr. Charles Kremer, a Romanian American dentist, discovered that Trifa had come to the United States. Many of Kremer's Jewish family members had been killed during a riot in Romania in 1941. Kremer sent scores of documents to the US government claiming that Trifa was responsible for this crime and other crimes during World War II. Kremer pressed the government for years to prosecute Trifa.

Finally, in 1975, the US Justice Department began investigating Trifa for committing war crimes. Among other charges, federal officials said that Trifa had lied on his citizenship papers. They claimed Trifa had been a Nazi sympathizer. He had been a member of the Romanian Iron Guard, a violent pro-Nazi political movement dedicated to driving Jews out of Romania. Officials stated that in 1941 Trifa had made an anti-Semitic speech in Romania. The speech had sparked four days of attacks in which more than three hundred Jews and other Romanians were killed, including Charles Kremer's relatives. However, in order to deport (or expel) Trifa from the United States, federal officials had to prove their case.

The West German government sent the US Justice Department documents tying Trifa to Nazi

Valerian Trifa, pictured here in 1982, could no longer deny his past after the discovery of fingerprint evidence that linked him to a 1942 postcard in which the author pledged loyalty to the Nazi party.

crimes. One intriguing piece of evidence was a postcard that Trifa had allegedly written to a high-ranking Nazi official, Heinrich Himmler—the head of the Nazi SS (the German combat arm of the Nazi Party)—in 1942. The postcard was signed "Viorel Trifa," which was how Trifa was known in the church. In the postcard, Trifa pledged his loyalty to the Nazi party. Nevertheless, Trifa denied writing the card.

There had to be more proof. If Trifa had written the postcard, could it still have his fingerprints on it? The West German government refused to allow the FBI to use any techniques that might destroy this historic piece of evidence. So the FBI Identification Division used a new technique—a laser—to scan the postcard for latent fingerprints. Shockingly, the laser revealed a single thumbprint that had been preserved—and had gone unnoticed—for several decades.

Because a person's fingerprints never change, and because fingerprints can remain intact on a surface for years, the FBI was able to match the fingerprint on the postcard to Trifa's fingerprints that had been taken when he became a US citizen. The thumbprint on the postcard was among the most critical pieces of evidence tying Trifa to his past.

Trifa continually denied he had played a role in the attacks against Jews. When shown a photograph of himself wearing an Iron Guard uniform, he admitted to being a member of the group. He also admitted to working on an anti-Semitic newspaper and giving pro-Nazi speeches.

Yet Trifa never apologized for his actions. He told a reporter in 1973, "I am not ashamed of my past at all."[2] In 1980, hoping to avoid a trial, Trifa agreed to give up his US citizenship. The government, however, persisted. In the middle of a trial before an immigration judge in Detroit, Trifa voluntarily agreed to be deported. He claimed that he did so because the trial was placing a heavy financial burden on his church. When the deportation agreement was read, Charles Kremer was present in the courtroom. Trifa was deported from the United States to Portugal in 1984. He died of a heart attack in 1987 at the age of seventy-two.

Investigators can use all sorts of tricks and techniques to find fingerprints and identify suspects, even when those fingerprints are invisible or from years and years ago. The science behind solving crimes is becoming more and more advanced every day, and criminals are more and more likely to get caught. Therefore, some people have gone to great lengths to try to prevent investigators from using fingerprints to catch them. Unfortunately for them, they rarely ever find success.

CHAPTER 3

HOW CRIMINALS ATTEMPT TO EVADE FINGERPRINT IDENTIFICATION

It sometimes seems like there is no way to escape being fingerprinted. As Trifa's case shows, a person's crimes can catch up with them years, even decades later, thanks to fingerprint identification, and the technology is only becoming more effective. Yet criminals still try hard to hide their prints, sometimes with gloves, and sometimes with far more painful methods. Unluckily for them and happily for law enforcement, these methods often prove ineffective.

Gloves are one of the seemingly easiest way to disguise a person's fingerprints. In 1962 two

Criminals may try to wear rubber gloves to hide their fingerprints, but scientists can now sometimes identify latent fingerprints people leave even when wearing gloves.

thieves stole famous paintings from a London art gallery. The robbers thought they had outwitted police by wearing rubber gloves. However, they tossed the packaging from their gloves into a trashcan. They never thought that police would search the trash and find their fingerprints on the packaging. Today, thanks to advanced fingerprint technology, scientists can sometimes even identify the latent prints left by gloved hands.

In another account, a gang of thieves who had carried out a series of robberies had rented an apartment. They were very careful to wipe down counters and other surfaces throughout the apartment to erase their fingerprints. They even loaded the dishwasher to scrub their fingerprints off their plates and glasses. The only problem: they forgot to turn on the dishwasher. Their fingerprints were easily identified on the unwashed dishware, and they were soon caught.

Bloody Extremes

Sometimes criminals go to unbelievable extremes to "erase" their fingerprints and avoid being caught. Some have tried rubbing their fingertips with sandpaper to rub off their prints. Others resort to even more brutal methods, such as burning off their fingerprints with acid or even using surgery to slice them off. What's worse for these criminals (but good for law enforcement) is that these gruesome and painful methods usually don't work. Ridges in fingerprints run deep into the skin. Since skin is always repairing itself, fingerprints usually grow back in the same patterns. Even if the prints don't grow back completely, the scars left behind create new characteristics for an examiner to trace.

Shockingly, the first time a criminal tried to destroy his fingerprints occurred just as fingerprinting was becoming a popular crime-solving technique. In England in 1907, a suspect exited a police wagon with blood dripping from his fingers. He had used a metal tag attached to his shoelace to slice the pads off his fingertips. The man had made a desperate attempt to avoid being identified. Scotland Yard was in a frenzy. Had the man just discovered a way to bypass their new identification system? Would other criminals follow his lead? Fingerprint experts waited anxiously for weeks while the suspect's fingers healed. Luckily, the ridges on the thief 's fingertips grew back in the same patterns as before. His prints matched a set already on record. The man was convicted and sent to jail as a repeat criminal.

Public Enemy No. 1

Perhaps the most famous case of "fudging" fingerprints is that of John Dillinger, who escaped arrest so many times that in 1934 the FBI labeled him "Public Enemy No. 1." In the 1930s, Dillinger became known as a notorious bank robber and a murderer. During a crime spree that lasted several years, he robbed at least two dozen banks. With the help of his gang of fellow prisoners and girlfriends, he broke out of jail several times. During a holdup in 1934, Dillinger and his gang killed a Chicago police officer. Dillinger was sent to prison, but once again he broke free—and stole a sheriff 's car.

Dillinger would stop at nothing to avoid being caught. He even mutilated his own fingers! Some people claim that he tried to use acid to burn off his

John Dillinger, "Public Enemy Number One," is shown here at age thirty-one in 1934. He tried to evade capture by removing his fingerprints.

prints. Others say he paid a surgeon $5,000 to slice off the skin at the tips of his fingers and do some minor facial surgery.[1]

In 1934 a woman tipped off police to Dillinger's whereabouts. She told them that Dillinger would be seeing a movie at Chicago's Biograph Theater on July 22. The woman wore a red dress to signal the police. She later became known as "the lady in red." Police surrounded the theater. When they recognized Dillinger next to the lady in red, Dillinger pulled out a gun. Police shot and killed him next to the theater.

Because of Dillinger's reputation for eluding police, some people doubted that the man they had killed was in fact Public Enemy No. 1. To prove that they had nabbed the right man, examiners checked his fingerprints. They saw how badly he had damaged the skin at the tips of his fingers. However, some fingerprint ridges left untouched by the surgeon's scalpel (or unhurt by acid) were enough to make a match. Dillinger was definitely dead.

A Grisly Puzzle

People have gone to great lengths to disguise their fingertips, from slicing them off with razors to burning them with fire or acid. These painful methods often don't work because fingerprints grow back in the same or very similar patterns. One way criminals have tried to get around this is by transplanting skin from elsewhere on the body

Dead Prints

Sometimes investigators need to fingerprint a dead body to identify it. Depending on the manner of death and how long the person has been dead, this can require extra measures. For example, when skin dries out, it shrivels. That makes fingerprinting a mummified corpse nearly impossible. To soften up the skin, investigators may soak the fingertips in water or heat them with a microwave. Sometimes they inject the fingertips with chemical "tissue builder" to plump them up. If a body was in water for a long time, the skin can be badly damaged. In this case, an investigator may peel the skin off the dead person's fingers and then wear the skin like a glove to make a print.

onto the fingerprints to avoid their growing back the same way.

In 1990 police in Miami arrested a suspect in a drug case. They made a gruesome discovery: the man had sliced up his fingertips and had tried to transplant pieces of skin onto other fingers. When his fingers healed, he was left with bizarrely jagged prints. Ridges ran in all directions. No match could be

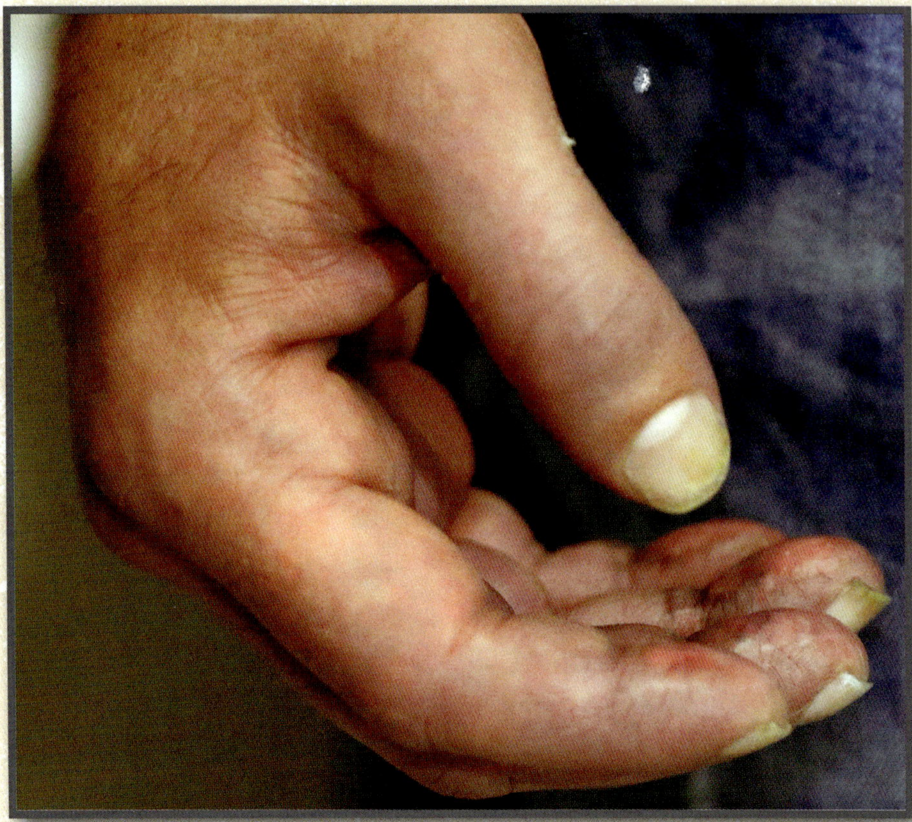

A criminal wanted for drug trafficking and murder removed his fingerprints. This close-up shows his mutilated fingertips.

made using the FBI's computerized fingerprint database. Then, a fingerprint specialist had an ingenious idea. He printed photos of the suspect's butchered prints. Then he cut the photos and carefully pasted them back together like pieces of a jigsaw puzzle. The reassembled prints matched those of a man convicted in another drug case. Case solved.

New Technology on Both Sides

Since September 11, 2001, police at border patrols have seen a new trend of people going to extremes to remove their fingerprints. This may be a response to post-9/11 efforts by the Department of Homeland Security to beef up security at border crossings. In addition to installing more security cameras and hiring more agents, Homeland Security officials have been fingerprinting every non-resident entering the United States. They run the prints through NGI's AFIT system. The prints are compared with a list of the most-wanted criminals and the FBI's terrorist watch list to see if they can find a match.

In May 2006, border police in New Mexico arrested a Jamaican man who was facing charges

Born Without Fingerprints

Surprisingly, some people never develop fingerprints at all! Two very rare genetic disorders—Naegeli syndrome and dermatopathia pigmentosa reticularis (DPR)—have a very unusual effect: they make a person's fingertips as smooth as glass.

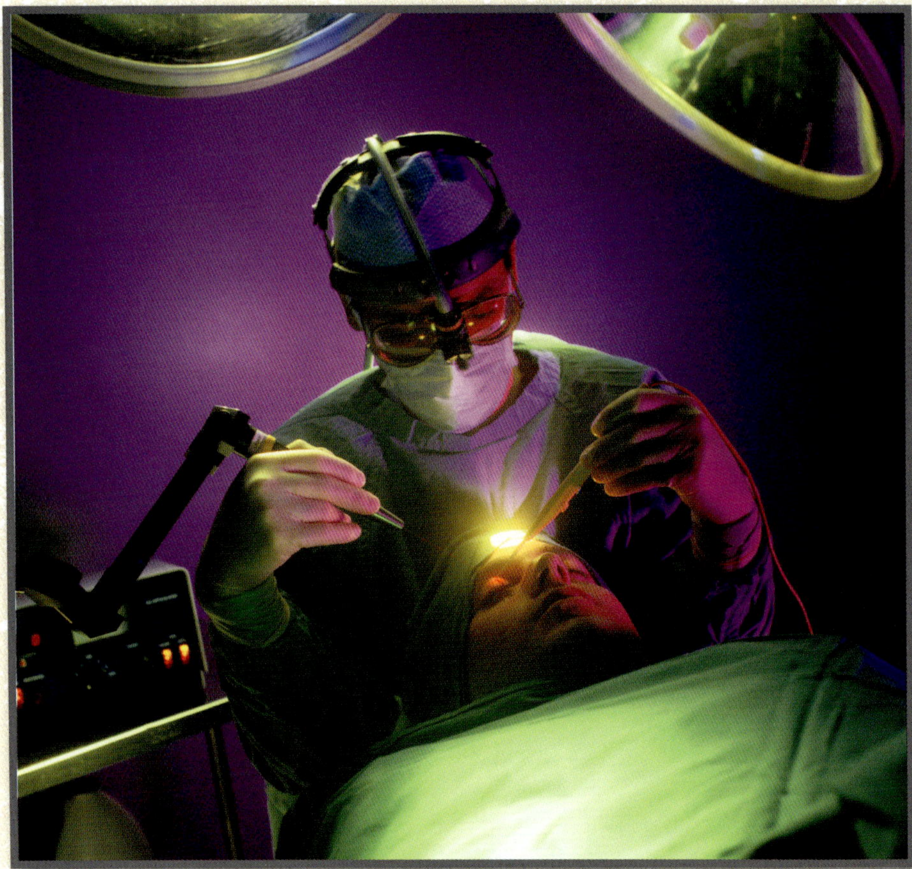

A plastic surgeon uses a dermal laser. Lasers can be used for chemical peeling, dermabrasion, laser surgery, and even to attempt to destroy fingerprints.

of handling money illegally (money laundering). They noticed that the man's fingertips were healing from surgery. He was also limping at the time of his arrest. The man had apparently paid a surgeon to replace his fingerprints with skin from his feet! The man's painful surgery failed, and his surgeon was arrested, too.

New surgical technology can make law enforcement officials anxious. Dermal lasers, like those used for plastic surgery, could be used to alter fingerprints at a deeper level so that they grow pack differently. More effective transplants could make it more and more difficult to identify people who have had their fingerprints surgically altered.[2]

Yet technology helps police departments as well. New identification tools, such as facial recognition software, can be used in conjunction with partial fingerprints or palm prints to identify someone

A biometric scanner uses the shape and planes of this man's face to match him against database records to identify him.

with mangled fingertips. These new technologies also help by making fingerprinting identification more accurate. The fingerprinting process, though effective, isn't always foolproof. Biometrics and other identification technologies that might help when there are no fingerprints available can also make identification more accurate when fingerprints are available, leading to fewer arrests of innocent people.

CHAPTER 4

WHEN FINGERPRINTS LEAD TO THE WRONG CONVICTION

Because every person's fingerprint is unique, fingerprinting is a highly useful method of connecting criminals to their crimes and has been for more than a century. Yet fingerprint analysis is not perfect, and mistakes do happen. Technology can help narrow down the number of suspects from a national—even global—pool, but the it is up to human examiners to confirm whether or not two prints truly match. Machines aren't smart enough yet to make those final connections. However, this means that every time fingerprints are matched there is some potential for human error.

According to Simon Cole, associate professor of criminology (the study of crime and criminals) at the University of California, Irvine, the question isn't whether two fingerprints from different people could ever look exactly alike. The question is whether the prints of two random individuals could appear close enough to throw off a fingerprint expert. Many fingerprints that are lifted from crime scenes are smudged. Very often they are only partial prints, tiny fragments of a complete fingerprint. Even with the wide variety of techniques used to lift prints at a crime scene and the advanced technology used in crime labs to match prints, mistakes can be made. Following are two flawed-fingerprint cases in which innocent people spent time in jail for crimes they did not commit.

Mistaken in Madrid

During the peak of rush hour, on the morning of March 11, 2004, disaster struck. A series of bombings ripped through four commuter trains in Madrid, Spain. The bombs had been detonated in backpacks stowed on the trains. The explosions killed 191 people. As many as 2,051 others were injured by the blasts.

While searching for the terrorists who had committed these attacks, Spanish police uncovered a partial latent fingerprint on a plastic bag that contained detonators. For help with their investigation, they sent digital images of the print to the FBI. US officials ran the prints through IAFIS, the FBI's computerized database. The database produced a short list of potential matches. Three FBI fingerprint experts determined that the print belonged to a man named Brandon Mayfield, a lawyer living in Oregon.

Police officers in Madrid examine the wreckage left by the March 11, 2004, bombings.

Mayfield's prints were on file because of a burglary arrest in 1984, when he was a teenager. The FBI apparently found fifteen points of comparison (or ridge characteristics) between the partial print from the bombings and Mayfield's fingerprint. US officials called the match a "bingo match."[1] A fourth fingerprint examiner agreed with the match.

Mayfield was arrested as a material witness to the bombings. During a raid on Mayfield's home, the FBI took his computers, modem, safe-deposit key, papers, and copies of the Koran, a sacred Muslim text (Mayfield was a convert to Islam), as well as "Spanish documents." These later turned out to be the homework of one of Mayfield's sons.

Soon after Mayfield's arrest, Spanish authorities alerted the FBI that they had made a terrible mistake. The print actually belonged to an Algerian man named Ouhnane Daoud. Mayfield had absolutely no ties to the bombings. In fact, he hadn't left the United States in ten years. He was released after spending two weeks in jail. All of his property was returned to him. He described his time in jail as "humiliating" and "embarrassing."[2] When other inmates learned about his suspected terrorist ties, he had feared for his safety.

Mayfield later sued the US Justice Department for their serious blunder. In November 2006, he was awarded a two-million-dollar settlement. He also received an apology from the Justice Department and the FBI as well as an agreement that the FBI

Brandon Mayfield sits at a press conference in 2004 in Portland, Oregon. He was exonerated after the FBI was alerted by Spanish authorities that Mayfield's arrest had been a mistake.

would destroy any conversations they had recorded from his home and office during the investigation.

Liberated by New Evidence

On May 30, 1997, after a struggle with an unknown attacker, Boston police officer Sergeant Gregory Gallagher was shot with his own gun in the backyard of a house. The attacker also fired a shot at a witness watching from a second-story window. Running from the scene, the shooter left behind a baseball cap. Then he forced his way into a nearby home and drank water from a glass mug. He fled that home as well, leaving behind the gun and a white sweatshirt that he had worn.

About two weeks later, the injured police officer looked at mug shots of possible suspects. He picked a man named Stephan Cowans as the shooter. He later chose Cowans out of a lineup, a group of people lined up by police for identification by witnesses to a crime. The witness from the upstairs window also selected Cowans from a lineup. Yet the family who lived in the house that the attacker had entered did not identify Cowans.

Nevertheless, at the trial, the jury relied on the testimony of Sergeant Gallagher and that of the upstairs neighbor. Jurors also focused on a latent fingerprint that was found on the glass that the attacker had used. Fingerprint experts claimed that the fingerprint belonged to Cowans. He was convicted on numerous counts, including assault

In 2004 Stephan Cowans was released after serving time in prison for a crime he did not commit. Experts made an error when they said the perpetrator's fingerprint matched Cowans's.

and battery of a police officer, home invasion, and battery by means of a dangerous weapon. He was sentenced to thirty to forty-five years in prison.

On May 22, 2003, new evidence surfaced in the case. At the request of Cowans's lawyer, the Suffolk Superior Court issued a release of the key pieces of evidence: the glass mug, swabs taken from the mug, the baseball cap, and the sweatshirt. All of the evidence was tested for DNA. Stephan Cowans's DNA did not match the DNA on these items. In addition, a re-examination of the fingerprint found on the drinking glass proved that it did not belong to Cowans. He could not have been the attacker.

On January 23, 2004, Stephan Cowans walked out of prison a free man. He had served five and a half years for a crime he did not commit. The real attacker is still at large.

Make Way for DNA

Today, many people are becoming skeptical about the accuracy of fingerprint analysis. Cases like these bring several flaws to the forefront. First, questions arise as to who can be considered a fingerprint expert. All fingerprint examiners go through training, which can take several months. An organization called the International Association for Identification gives a certifying exam to fingerprint examiners. However, many crime labs—including the FBI lab—do not require certification for officers to identify fingerprints. In addition, judges do not require that fingerprint examiners who testify in court be certified. The bottom line, critics say, is that fingerprint analysis is based on human judgment, and all humans make mistakes.

Another major problem with fingerprint analysis, according to Jennifer L. Mnookin, a professor at the UCLA School of Law, is that it is not an exact science.[3] In court, a fingerprint expert can testify that a match is certain. Yet that claim cannot be proven. Studies have never been completed to demonstrate how often two random people could have similar fingerprints. After more than a century of fingerprint analysis, many questions still remain unanswered. How often do similar fingerprints confuse examiners? What about partial prints? Can small fragments of two different people's prints be the same? This information remains unknown.

Some people believe that fingerprint analysis will soon be replaced by DNA analysis. Introduced in the 1980s, DNA profiling has revolutionized forensic science. Unlike fingerprint comparison, DNA profiling developed over the past few decades through extensive biological research at top-notch academic centers. Every person who is not an identical twin has unique DNA. According to the FBI, when DNA evidence is presented at trial, their experts can testify with 99 percent certainty that a specific individual—and no other person in the country—is the source of the DNA.[4] As of now, a good deal of fingerprint evidence cannot be presented with the same degree of certainty.

A person's DNA is the same in every cell of the body that has a nucleus (such as skin, muscle, and nerve cells). A lab needs only thirty to fifty microscopic cells to make a match. Today's highly sensitive equipment may even be able to make a match with

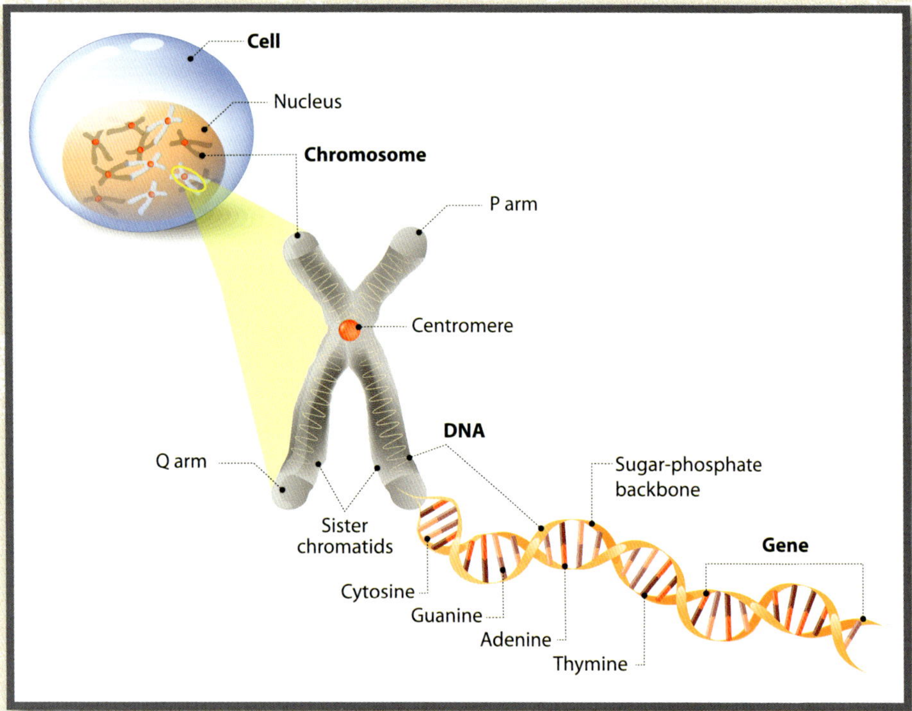

The DNA molecule is in the shape of a double helix, and strands of DNA make up genes. Genes code for specific proteins that help the cells perform a certain function.

as few as six cells. However, the admissibility in court of such small samples has not been established.

DNA can be collected in minute traces—from blood, saliva, sweat, hair, and body tissues. It can even be lifted from skin cells left in a fingerprint. When a person is tied to a crime through DNA, there are reliable statistics—and a significant amount of scientific data—to back up that claim. In addition, even in small amounts, DNA has a set structure. It can be digitized and analyzed on computers.

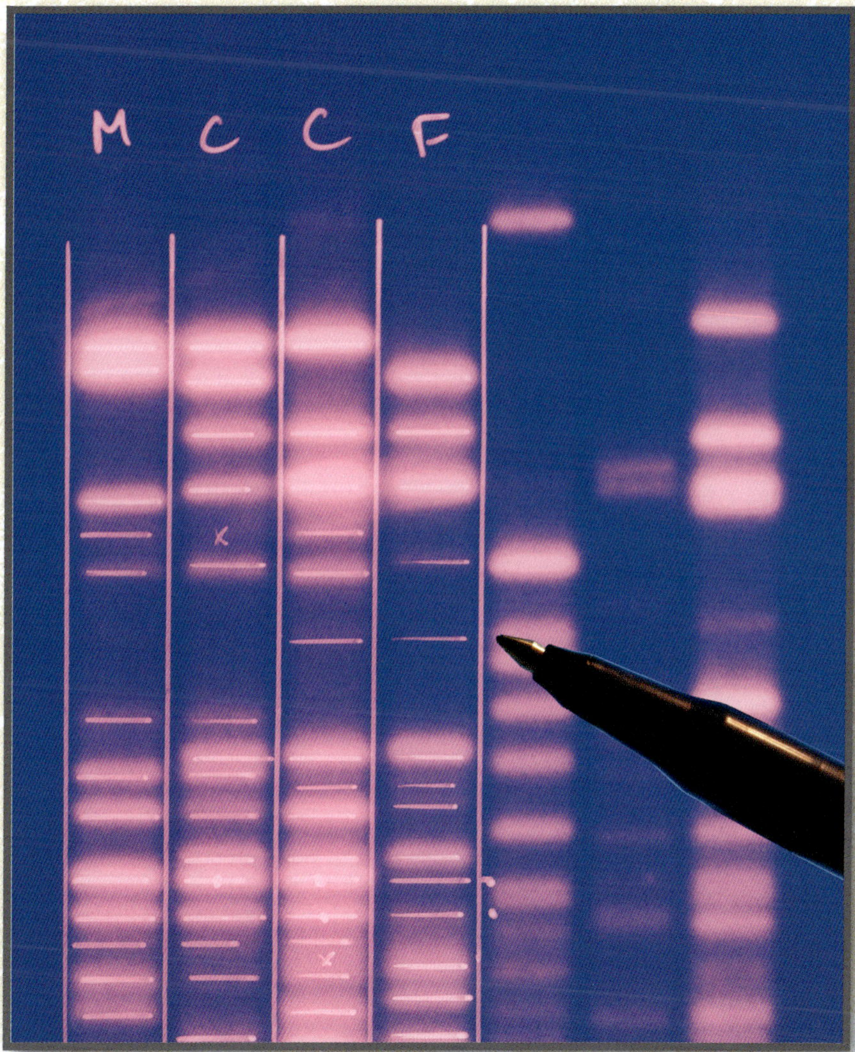

This autoradiograph shows bands of DNA belonging to a mother (M), father (F), and two children (C). Each individual possesses these bands in a unique pattern, so they're called DNA fingerprints. If two DNA samples match perfectly, they belong to the same person. If the samples have some of the bands in common, the two people are at least related.

Certainty and Statistics

Historically, fingerprint evidence has always been presented with certainty in a courtroom. Either the fingerprints match or they don't. Some people have suggested that fingerprinting experts be allowed to express a degree of certainty or uncertainty about the match because fingerprints that don't perfectly match may still prove valuable to the case. One statistical model developed by Cedric Neumann, a professor of statistics at South Dakota State University, would "help forensic experts grade the quality of crime scene fingerprints and calculate the probability that a print found at a crime scene was left by a particular person."[5]

Neumann's method involves likelihood ratios, or a comparison between two values, which are already used in DNA cases with mixed samples. Furthermore, DNA experts can say that the DNA matches up to a certain percentage, so why can't fingerprint experts say, for example, that the fingerprint matches at a certain number of points of comparison? This might reduce the number of cases in which innocent people go to jail thanks to print identification mistakes. Opponents of this strategy claim that bringing up points might confuse a jury.

Fingerprints taken from a crime scene can be much fuzzier. A smudged print, for example, may reveal a tiny segment of a ridge pattern, with very few points of comparison. A clear copy of the same print, meanwhile, will have many more points of comparison. Other factors play a role in the quality of a fingerprint, such as the surface that the print was found on (for example, paper or glass) or the pressure of the fingers that created the print.

Yet just as fingerprints can be fuzzy, DNA can be contaminated. Neither is a perfect system, and although fingerprint matches are made by fallible humans rather than computer systems, it is often incredibly accurate. A 2010 study found that expert fingerprint examiners incorrectly identified a positive match between two prints only .01% of the time, leading to a 99.8% accuracy rate.[6] It seems doubtful that anyone would stop using such an effective system simply because other identification systems exist. Instead, it would make sense to use DNA identification, fingerprinting, and other biometrics together to independently confirm and reinforce the accuracy of identifications.

CHAPTER 5

NEXT GENERATION IDENTIFICATION AND BEYOND

Humans have known fingerprints are unique for millennia, but it is only in the past hundred years that they have been used to help solve crimes. In recent years, however, they've come to do far more than that.

Picture this scenario. You're standing at the entrance to Disney's Magic Kingdom. The line seems to go on forever. You can't wait to buy your ticket and head over to the rides in Tomorrowland. As you enter the park, the attendant asks you to scan your fingerprints. Are you busted? What's going on?

Since 2006, visitors at Disney World's four Orlando theme parks have been asked to scan their fingerprints at the entrance. According to park officials, this measure allows them to

Even some gyms offer entry using fingerprint scanners to confirm that everyone who walks in is a member.

protect against ticket fraud. If you buy a multiday pass, you are the only one who can use it. You are not permitted to resell your multiday ticket (which lowers the price of a daily pass) to make a profit. Fingerprints are an instant way to prove that you are you.

The Disney scenario is a stark reminder of how far fingerprint technology has come. For decades, police relied on ink pads and fingerprint cards to nab criminals. They slogged through hundreds—or thousands—of fingerprint cards trying to make a match. Today, all you have to do is scan your fingerprint and you're in the system.

The Beautiful World of Biometrics

Biometrics used to belong to spy movies and science fiction. The hero might put their palm to a pad and allow a computer to scan their eye, and at the time it seemed like a technological miracle. Yet what tourists at Disney World—and all of the rest of us—are witnessing today is the introduction of biometrics in everyday life. These systems are becoming more and more common in routine tasks. Today most smartphones can be unlocked using a fingerprint, and many apps, such as those used for banking or personal medical information, use fingerprints as well. Some apps even offer facial recognition and voice identification. Your fingerprint might also be required at ATMs, and can even be used as a payment method in some places, such as certain

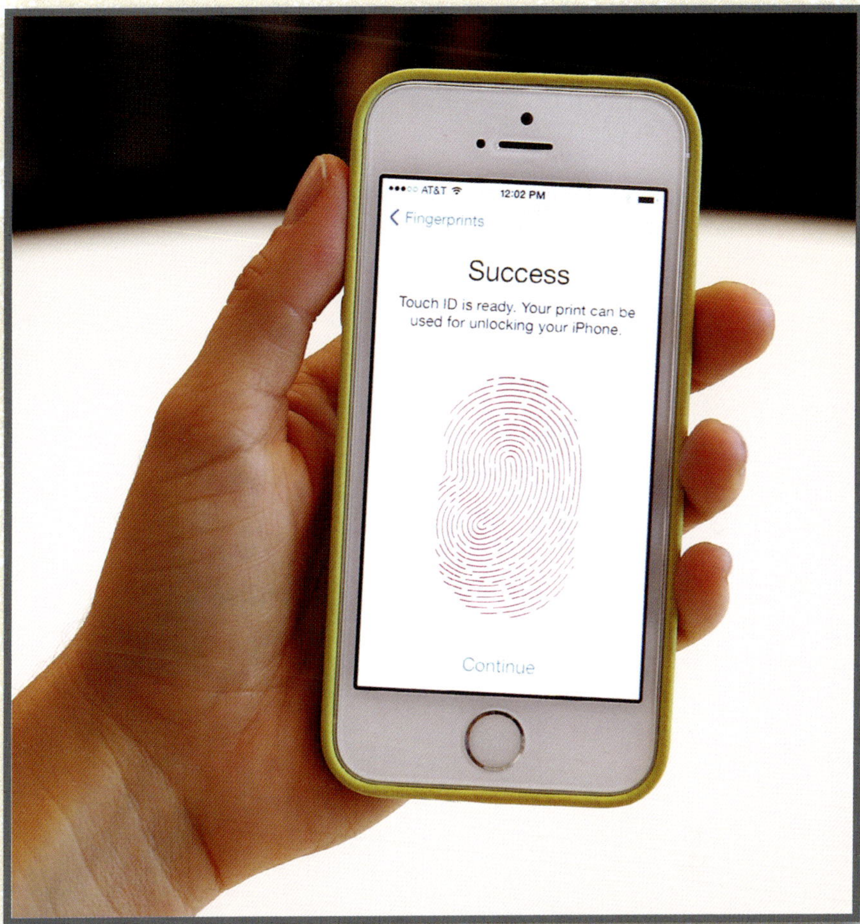

The iPhone 5S was the first iPhone model to use fingerprint recognition technology. All iPhone models following the 5S can be opened using fingerprints.

high school cafeterias. Fingerprints are an expected part of checking applicants' backgrounds for jobs at schools and in the government.

As you have seen, fingerprints have proven to be reliable sources of identification because they are, as far as we know, unique to each person, and

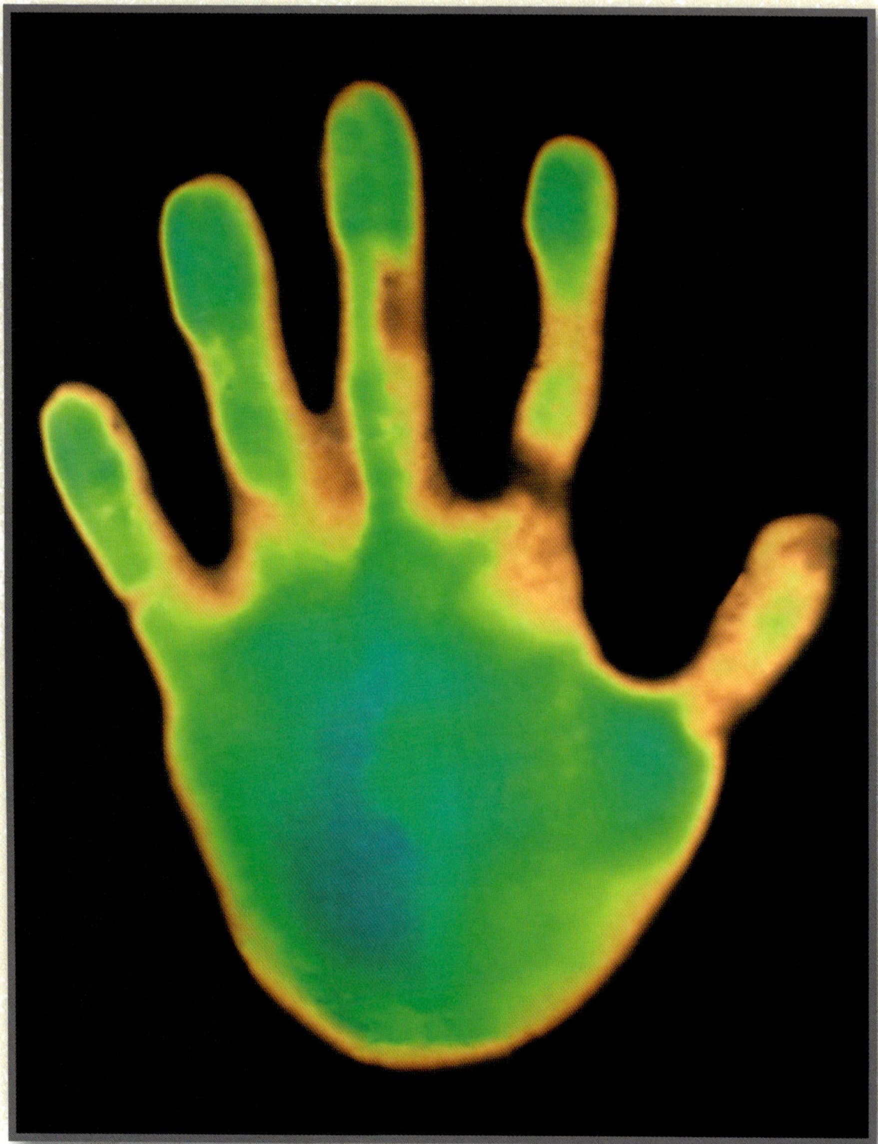

A thermogram is an image created using the heat radiating off an object. The orange indicates the warmest areas of the hand, while the blue shows the coldest areas. Thermography could be useful as a security measure in addition to fingerprints.

because they don't change over time. Being able to scan your fingerprints might also make life a bit easier: You won't have to remember to carry ID cards with you and you won't have to memorize multiple passwords or PINs.

Scientists, such as Anil K. Jain, a professor of computer science and engineering at Michigan State University, are working on programs to make fingerprinting technology more accurate. One challenge that Dr. Jain faces is designing biometric systems that can't be fooled. Say, for example, that someone uses a biometric system to protect a safe full of jewels. The safe has a scanner that recognizes the owner's fingerprint. A crafty thief might be able to lift the owner's print, make a plastic copy of it, and break into the safe. Researchers are now developing systems containing sensors that detect body heat and other signs of life. In addition, Jain notes that systems that recognize multiple traits (for example, ten prints instead of one, or faces in addition to fingerprints) tend to be more accurate and reliable.

What About Privacy?

As explained in chapter one, the FBI replaced their old fingerprinting system with a new system, Next Generation Identification, that keeps track of countless amounts of data, including advanced palm print identification and iris scans. What will the next iteration of this system include? Will it have records of people's gait, of their dental records, of their footprints? Their entire genomes?

New uses for fingerprint technology—from border crossings to theme park entries to school lunch lines—and the development of even more biometric technologies have people who want to protect privacy on high alert. They want to know who will have access to the data. What does your fingerprint tell someone about who you are, where you have been, or how you spend your time and money? What about facial recognition or DNA?

The question for everyone else becomes: at what point does a process that enhances security become an invasion of privacy? Are you willing to give up some privacy in order to be safe? Will the government or a private company be able to track you down wherever you are? Will people be under constant surveillance?

It seems as though people have largely accepted fingerprint technology as a matter of course—the convenience it introduces into people's lives makes it easy to forget privacy concerns. Facial recognition may be headed the same way. The program Snapchat and similar apps use facial recognition technology to alter images in funny ways, and almost everyone gets an ID photo taken at some point, whether for a driver's license, passport, or other document. We would be hard-pressed to keep our appearances a secret from the government.

A man has his photo taken for his driver's license. It is difficult to get by in the United States today without having some form of photo identification.

The biggest issues with privacy today have to do with DNA. While fingerprint technology can be used to identify someone, DNA can be used for far more. In particular, it tells scientists unprecedented amounts of information about things like a person's medical record and likelihood to fall prey to certain ailments. What's more, the analysis of DNA is still developing. One hundred years ago, we never would have expected fingerprints to be used for so many things—who knows what DNA might be able to tell us in the future?

Career Information

So you want to be a fingerprint expert? There are several levels of fingerprint expertise, each with its own duties, education requirements, and salary ranges. Learn more about the different job titles below.

JOB TITLE: Crime Scene Technician

Description: Detect, collect, and preserve physical evidence (including fingerprints) found at crime scenes; process and analyze fingerprints; photograph evidence; prepare evidence for submission to labs; maintain fingerprint records; conduct latent print examinations using AFIS; prepare crime scene reports for presentation in court

Education: Minimum of associate's degree in forensic science, biology, chemistry, criminal justice, or related field; experience in crime scene investigation, forensics, or related criminal justice work involving required skills, knowledge, and abilities

Salary range: $30,000–$49,000 (varies by experience and department)

JOB TITLE: Fingerprint Technician

Description: Take and process fingerprints, palm prints, and photographs of prisoners;

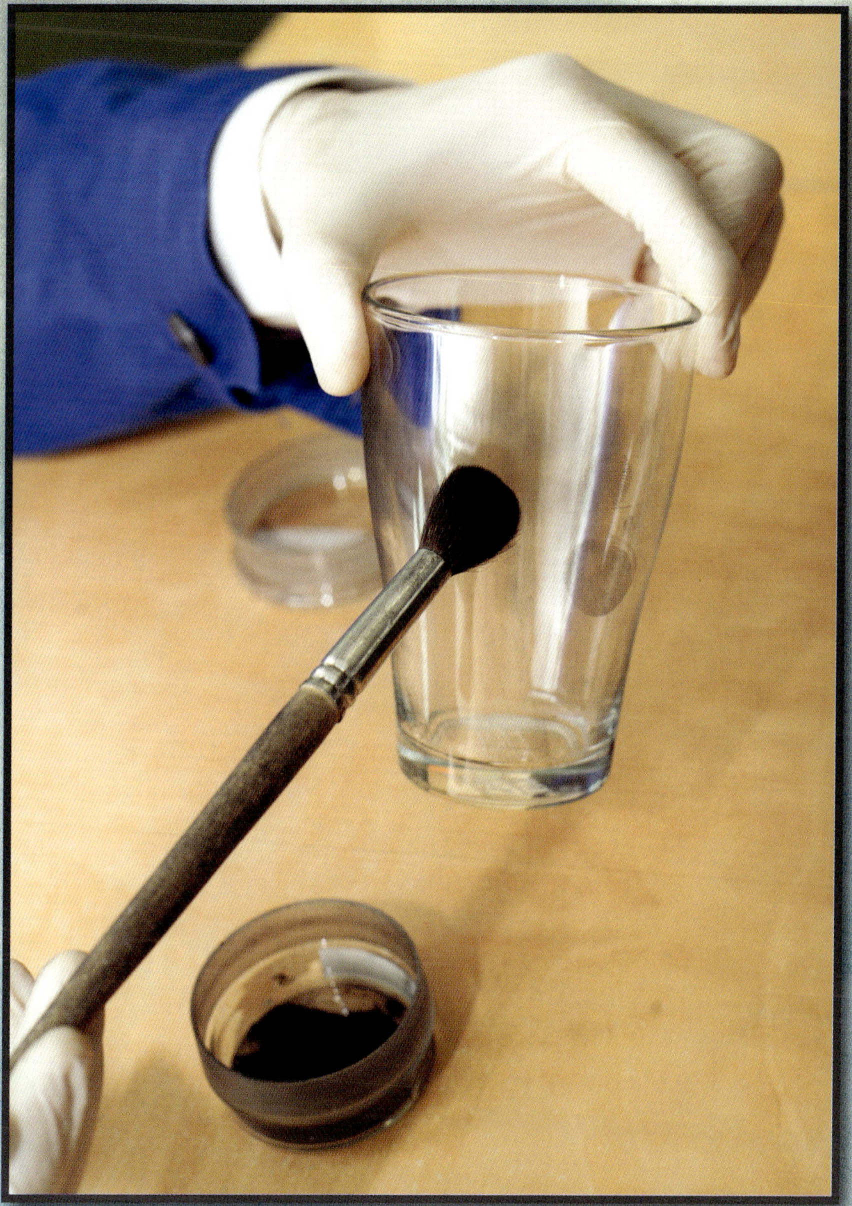

A fingerprint technician processes fingerprints from a glass. This is just one of several career options in fingerprint analysis.

use Live Scan and manual equipment to collect fingerprints and palm prints; transmit images through computer systems; identify basic ten prints; compare and classify physical details of fingerprints; maintain records

Education: Completion of formal or college-level course in fingerprint identification; at least six months in law enforcement in which duties include taking, classifying, and comparing fingerprints

Salary range: $35,000–$53,000 (varies by experience and department)

JOB TITLE: Latent Print Examiner/AFIS Technician

Description: Process fingerprint evidence collected at a crime scene or from an investigative agency (police, FBI, etc.); conduct latent print comparisons to determine identities for use in police investigations; operate computerized database searches; obtain prints from deceased people; testify in court

Education: College degree (bachelor of science in biology or chemistry preferred)

Certification (recommended, but not required): College degree; minimum two years of full-time experience as a latent print examiner; completion of certification exam

Average Salary: $44,000–$78,000 (may vary depending upon region, years of experience, and type of agency—local, state, or federal)

JOB TITLE: Latent Print Supervisor

Description: Supervise, assign, and evaluate work of technical personnel involved in latent print identification; train staff and police in latest methods and practices in fingerprint and related criminal identification work and in new laws, procedures, and policies in the field; train employees to use AFIS; compile and evaluate statistics regarding latent prints; provide expert witness testimony in court

Education: Minimum three years as latent print examiner (depending on department)

Average salary: $55,000–$88,000 (may vary depending upon region, years of experience, and type of agency—local, state, or federal)

JOB TITLE: Biometrics Engineer

Description: Create, or maintain systems for recording or processing biometrics, including fingerprints, facial identification, and voice recognition programs; develop and test biometric applications for use in law enforcement and security systems; research and design biometric software.

Education: College degree (bachelor of science in computer science or related field); computer language certification recommended; one-year graduate certificate in biometrics available.

Average salary: $80,000–$115,000 (may vary depending upon region, years of experience, and type of agency—local, state, or federal)

CHAPTER NOTES

INTRODUCTION: Not Quite Identical

1. Jeffery G. Barnes, "History" in *The Fingerprint Sourcebook* ed. International Association for Identification, et al. (National Institute of Justice, 2011), section 1.6, https://www.ncjrs.gov/pdffiles1/nij/235392.pdf.
2. Clay Dillow, "Enhancing Robots' Senses of Touch by Giving Them Human-Like Fingerprints," *Popular Science*, September 21, 2011, http://www.popsci.com/technology/article/2011-09/enhancing-robots-senses-touch-giving-them-human-fingerprints.
3. C. Claiborne Ray, "Twins and Fingerprints," *New York Times*, October 5, 2009, https://nyti.ms/2myb3V1.

CHAPTER 1. The History of Fingerprints

1. Jeffery G. Barnes, "History" in *The Fingerprint Sourcebook* ed. International Association for Identification, et al., (National Institute of Justice, 2011), sections 1.3–1.4, https://www.ncjrs.gov/pdffiles1/nij/235392.pdf.
2. Henry Faulds, *Nature*, vol.xxii, October 28, 1880, p. 605.
3. David Fisher, *Hard Evidence* (New York: Dell Publishing, 1996), p. 174.
4. Illinois Supreme Court, *People v. Jennings*, 252 Ill. 534, 96 N.E. 1077 (1911); Mark A. Acree, "*People v. Jennings:* A Significant Case in American Fingerprint

History," *The Print* 14.1 (1998), http://www.scafo.org/library/140401.html.

5. Federal Bureau of Investigation, "NGI Officially Replaces IAFIS—Yields More Search Options and Investigative Leads, and Increased Identification Accuracy," *CJIS Link* 16.2 (October 2014), https://www.fbi.gov/services/cjis/cjis-link/ngi-officially-replaces-iafis-yields-more-search-options-and-investigative-leads-and-increased-identification-accuracy.
6. Ibid.

CHAPTER 2. Picking Up Prints at the Scene of the Crime

1. David Fisher, *Hard Evidence* (New York: Dell Publishing, 1996), p. 169.
2. Ari L. Goldman, "Valerian Trifa, an Archbishop with a Fascist Past, Dies at 72," *New York Times*, January 29, 1987, p. B6.

CHAPTER 3. How Criminals Attempt to Evade Fingerprint Identification

1. David Fisher, *Hard Evidence* (New York: Dell Publishing, 1996), p. 175.
2. Anne-Marie Dornng, "Criminals Go to Painful Extremes to Mutilate Fingerprints," *ABC News*, July 26, 2010, http://abcnews.go.com/Technology/US/crooks-erase-past-erasing-fingerprints/story?id=11236512.

CHAPTER 4. When Fingerprints Lead to the Wrong Conviction

1. Jennifer L. Mnookin, "The Achilles' Heel of Fingerprints," *Washington Post,* May 29, 2004, p. A27.
2. The Associated Press, "FBI Apologizes to Lawyer in Bombing Case," *NBC News,* May 25, 2004, http://www.nbcnews.com/id/5053007/ns/us_news-security/t/fbi-apologizes-lawyer-held-madrid-bombings/#.WNxak6OZN0s
3. Jennifer L. Mnookin, "Fingerprints: Not a Gold Standard," *Issues in Science and Technology* (University of Texas at Dallas), October 9, 2003, http:www.issues.org/20.1/mnookin.html.
4. Bruce Budowle, Ranajit Chakaborty, George Carmody, and Keith L. Monson, "Source Attribution of a Forensic DNA Profile," *Journal of Forensic Science Communication,* vol. 2, no. 3, July 2000, https://archives.fbi.gov/archives/about-us/lab/forensic-science-communications/fsc/july2000/source.htm.
5. Douglas Page, "New Fingerprint Analysis Models Are at Hand," *Forensic Magazine,* August 28 2013, http://www.forensicmag.com/article/2013/08/new-fingerprint-analysis-models-are-hand.
6. Bradford T. Ulery, R. Austin Hicklin, JoAnn Buscaglia, and Maria Antonia Roberts, "Accuracy and Reliability of Forensic Latent Fingerprint Decisions," *PNAS 108.19,* May 10, 2011, http://www.pnas.org/content/108/19/7733.full.

GLOSSARY

arch A fingerprint pattern that slopes upward and downward like a hill.

biometrics Measurable characteristics that can be used for identification.

conviction A firm judgment as to whether someone is guilty or not of a crime.

dactylography The scientific study of fingerprints for the purpose of identification.

dactyloscopy The technique of taking someone's fingerprints.

distinct Different from something else in an obvious way.

DNA Short for deoxyribonucleic acid, it carries genetic information and exists in every cell.

evade To avoid.

fingerprint The pattern of ridges at the tip of a finger.

gait The way a person walks.

latent fingerprint A fingerprint that is not readily visible.

loop A fingerprint pattern that begins on one side of a fingertip, curves around, and exits on the other side.

minutiae Ridge details used to compare fingerprints.

patent fingerprint A fingerprint that is visible to the naked eye.

plastic fingerprint A 3D molded impression of a fingerprint found in soft materials such as soap, paint, or wet cement.

ridge A raised line of skin that forms a pattern at the tip of a finger.

whorl A spiral or circular fingerprint pattern.

FURTHER READING

Books

Anders, Mason. *DNA, Genes, and Chromosomes.* North Mankato, MN: Capstone Press, 2017.

Birmingham, Maria. *Biometrics: Your Body and the Science of Security.* Toronto: Owlkids Books, 2017.

Carmichael, L. E. *Discover Forensic Science.* Minneapolis, MN: Lerner Publishing, 2016.

Gardner, Robert, and Joshua Conklin. *Experiments for Future Forensic Scientists.* New York, NY: Enslow Publishing, 2017.

Libal, Angela. *Fingerprints, Bite Marks, Ear Prints.* Broomall, PA: Mason Crest, 2014.

Rauf, Don, and Judith Williams. *Forensic Science Specialists.* New York, NY: Enslow Publishing, 2015.

Websites

Crime Scene Investigator Network

www.crime-scene-investigator.net

Read articles on forensic science subjects, explore links to courses, and browse resources on how to become a crime scene investigator.

FBI, Friction Ridge Identification

recording-friction-ridges.s3-website-us-gov-west-1.amazonaws.com

This eLearning module from the FBI offers an interactive video tour through the process of recording and identifying fingerprints through friction ridges.

KidsAhead

kidsahead.com/subjects/10-crime-scene-investigation/activities

Read articles and do activities to learn more about crime scene investigation.

INDEX